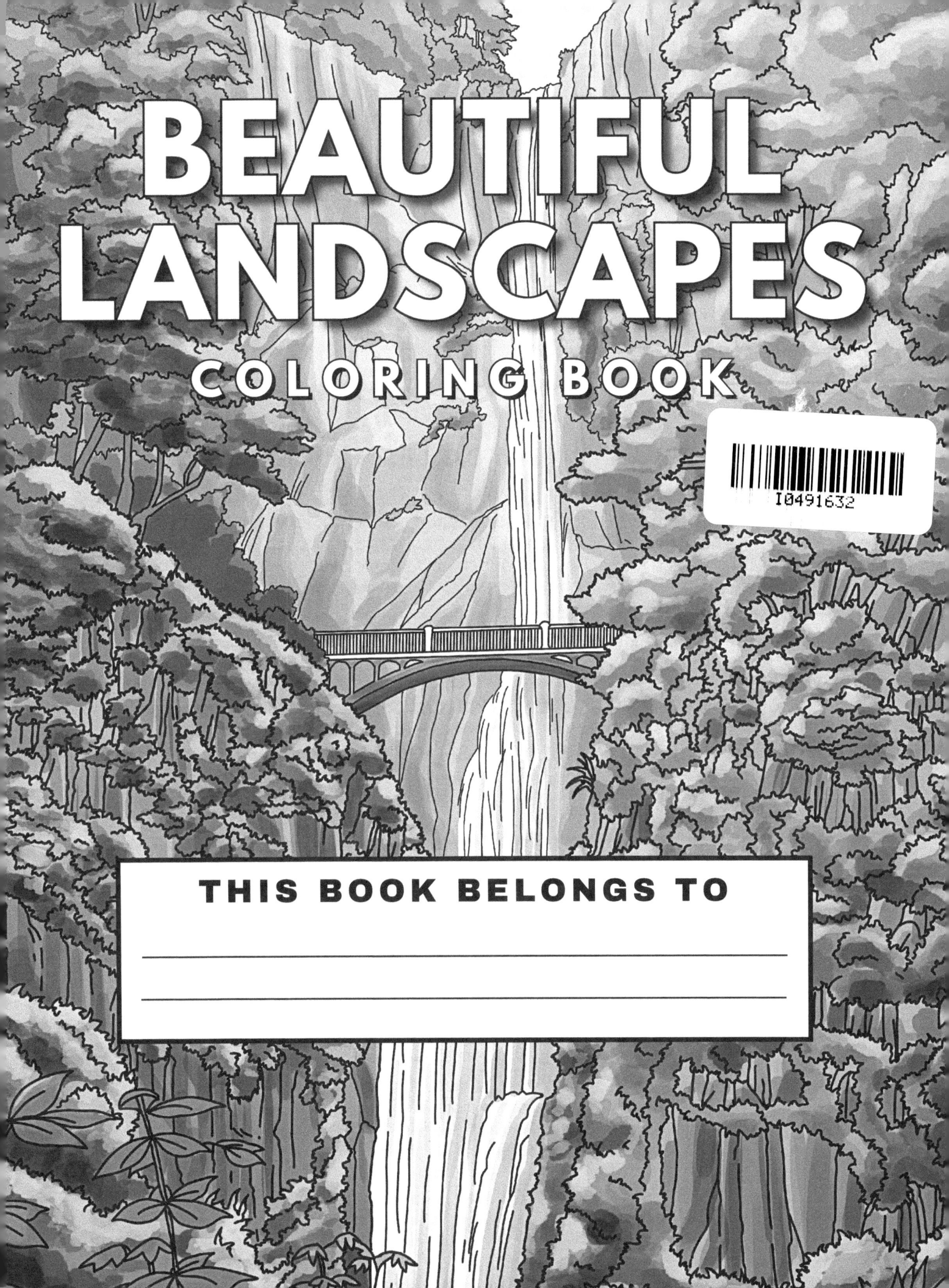

BEAUTIFUL
LANDSCAPES
COLORING BOOK

THIS BOOK BELONGS TO

A MESSAGE FROM THE PUBLISHER

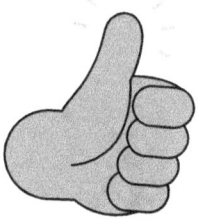

Hey, thank you for making the purchase, we really hope you enjoy this book. If you have the chance, then all feedback is greatly appreciated. We have put a lot of effort into making this book, so if you are not completely satisfied, please email us at ben@bclesterbooks.com and we will do our best to address the issues. If you have any suggestions, enquries or want to send us a selfie with this book, then email at the same address – ben@bclesterbooks.com

Is this book misprinted? Drop us an email with a photo of the misprint and we will send out another copy!

WHO ARE WE AT B.C. LESTER BOOKS?

B.C. Lester Books is a small publishing firm of three people based in Buckinghamshire, UK. We aim to provide quality works in all things geography, for kids and adults, with varying interests. We have already released a selection of activity, trivia and fact books and are working hard to bring you wider selection. Have a suggestion for us? Then email ben@bclesterbooks.com. We are all ears!

LOOKING FOR A SIMILAR COLORING EXPERIENCE?

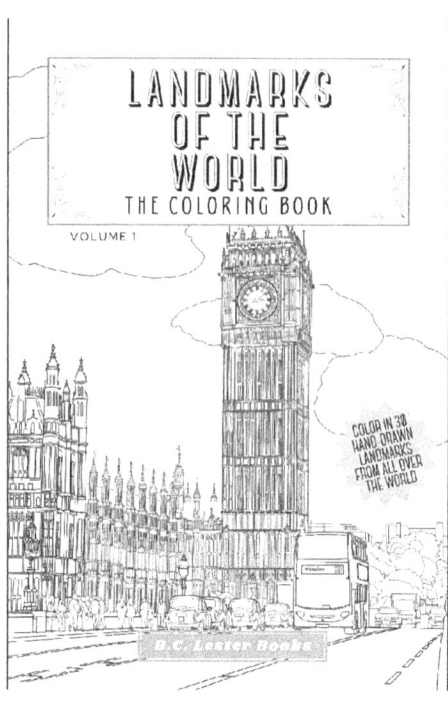
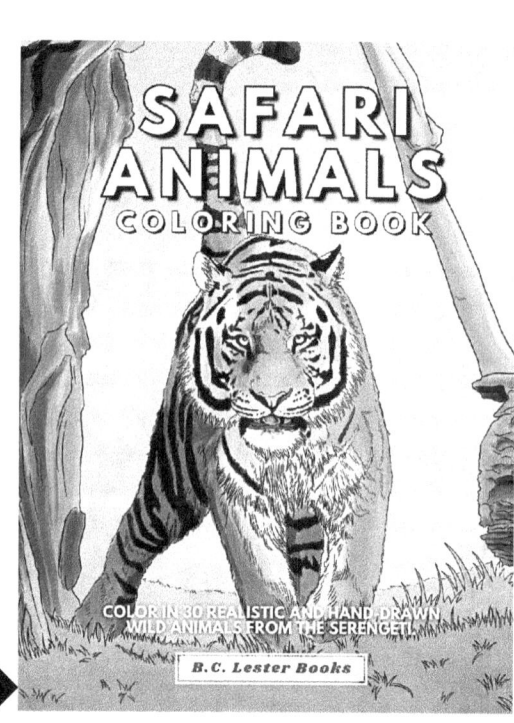

BEFORE YOU START...

Test your coloring equipment here for bleedthrough. Note that this coloring book is NOT recommended for paint, gel pens or highlighters...

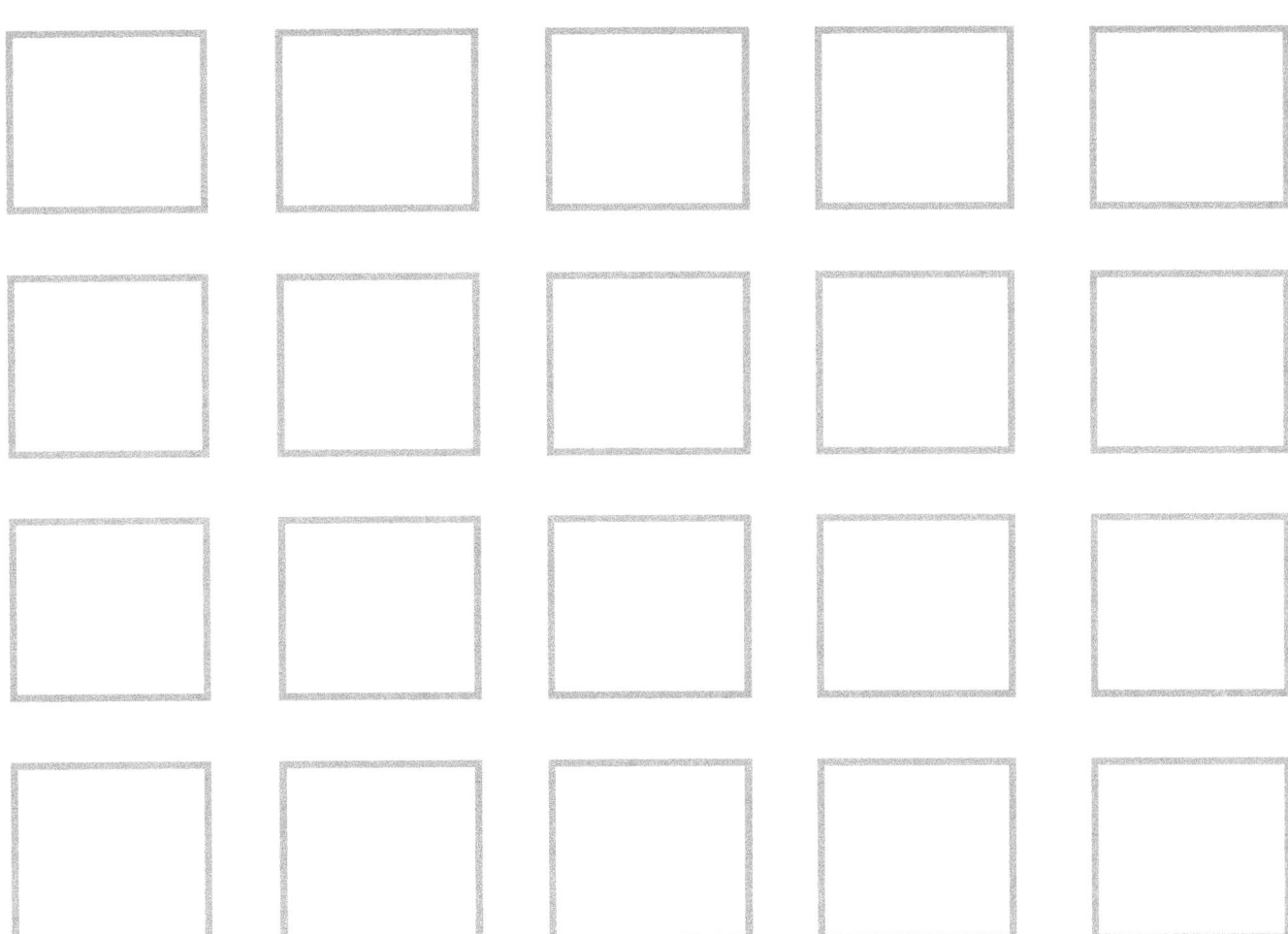

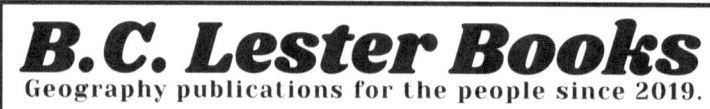

READY TO START?

Relax, unwind, and enjoy the experience!

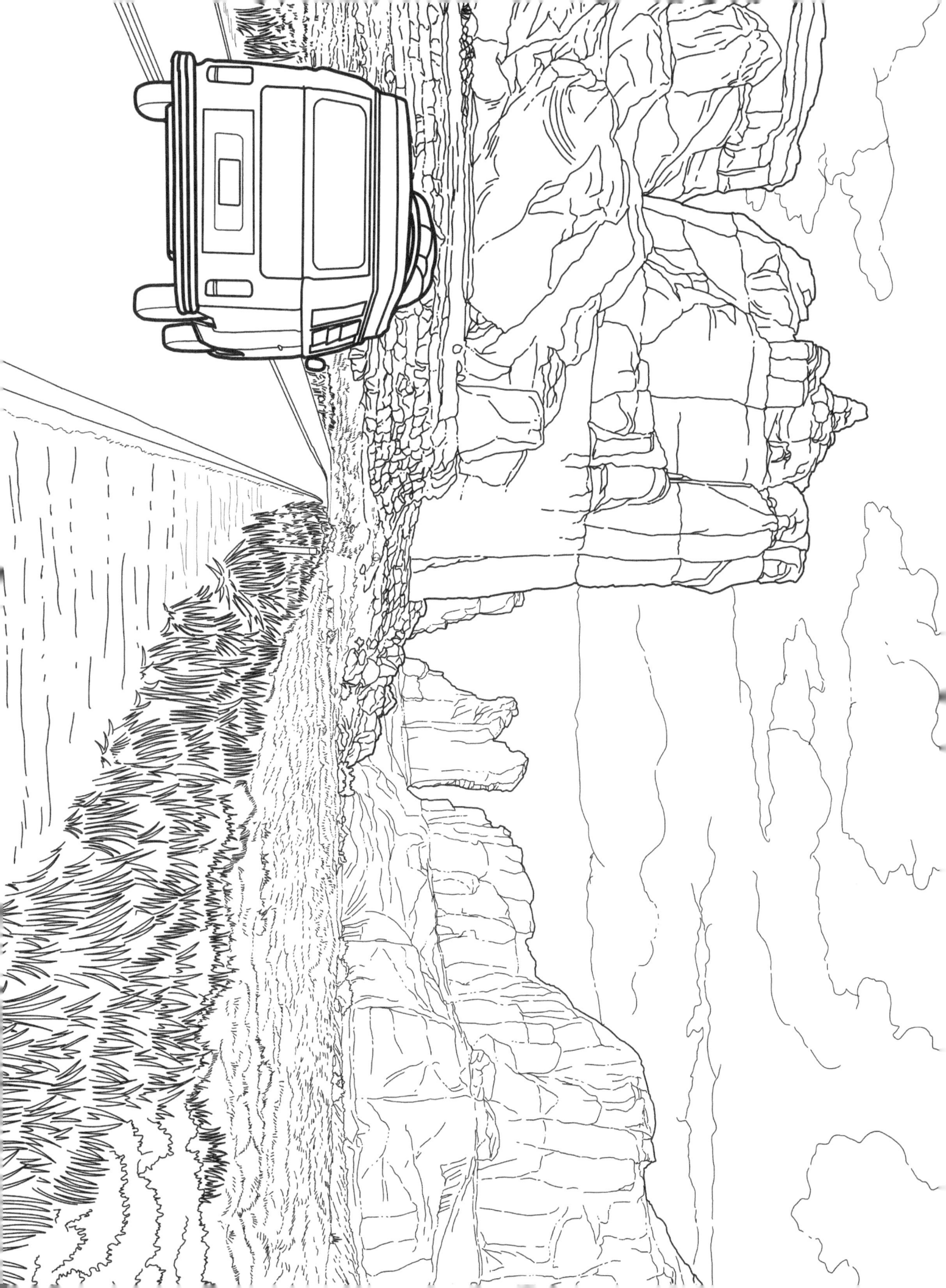

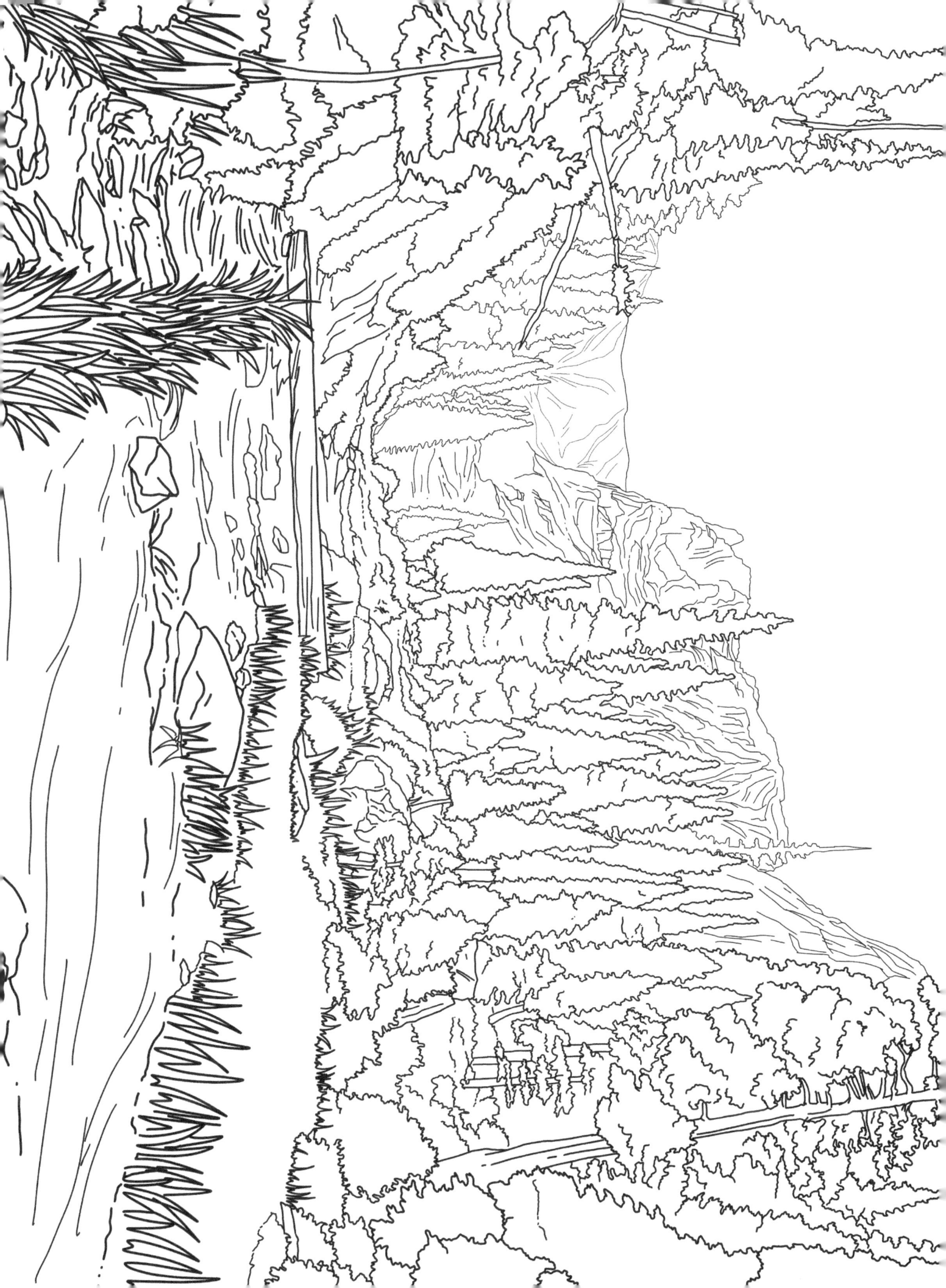

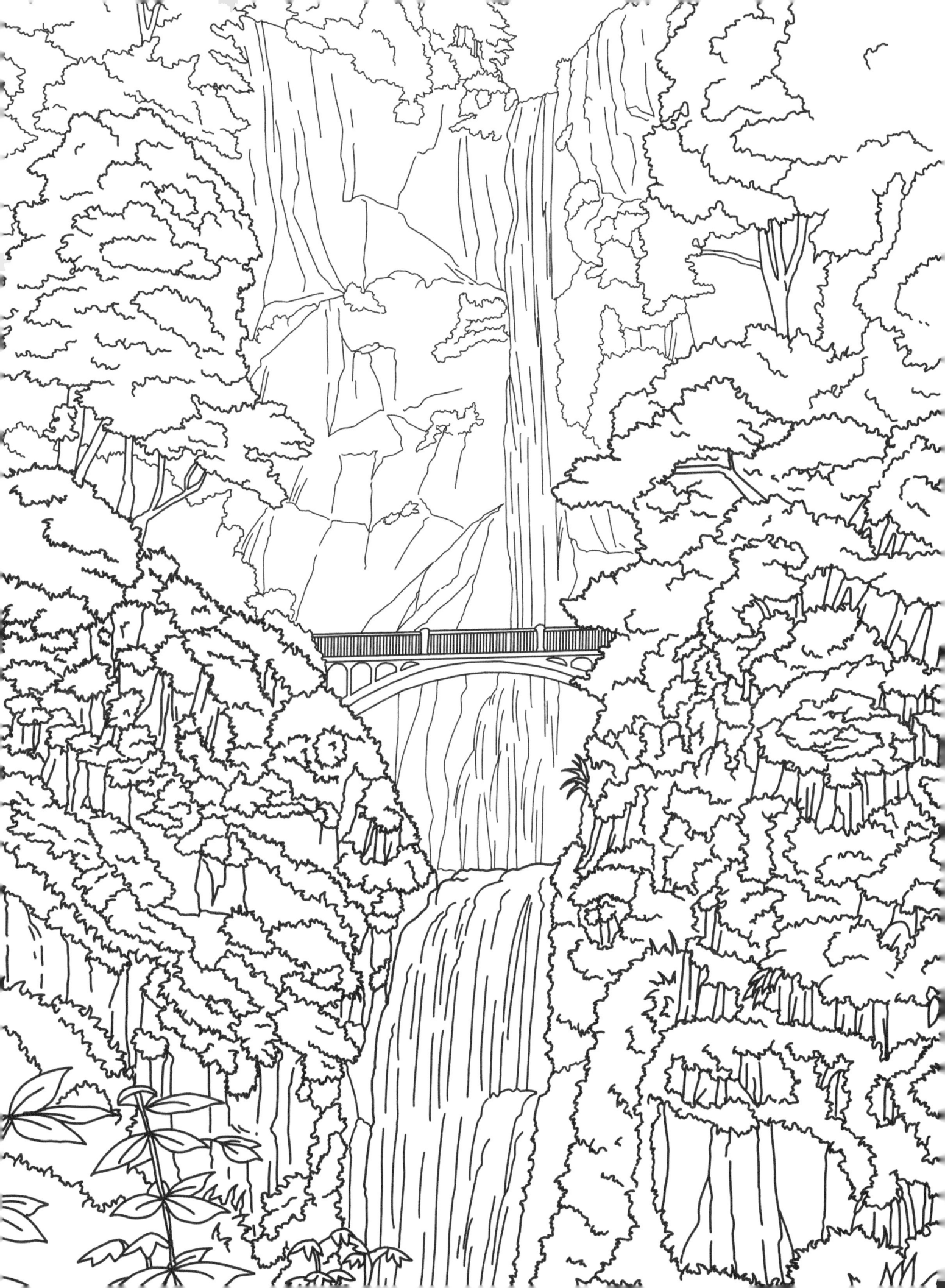

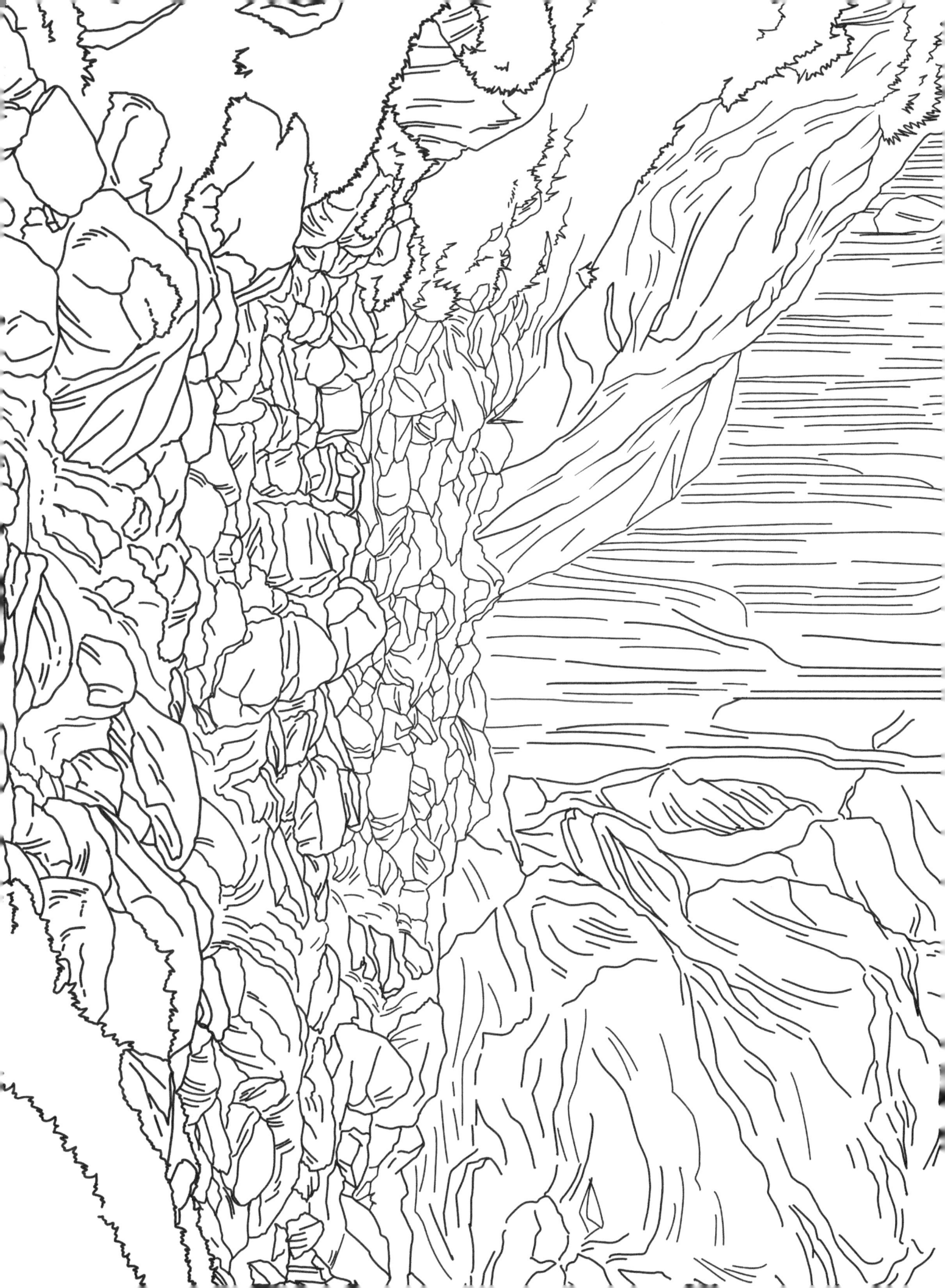

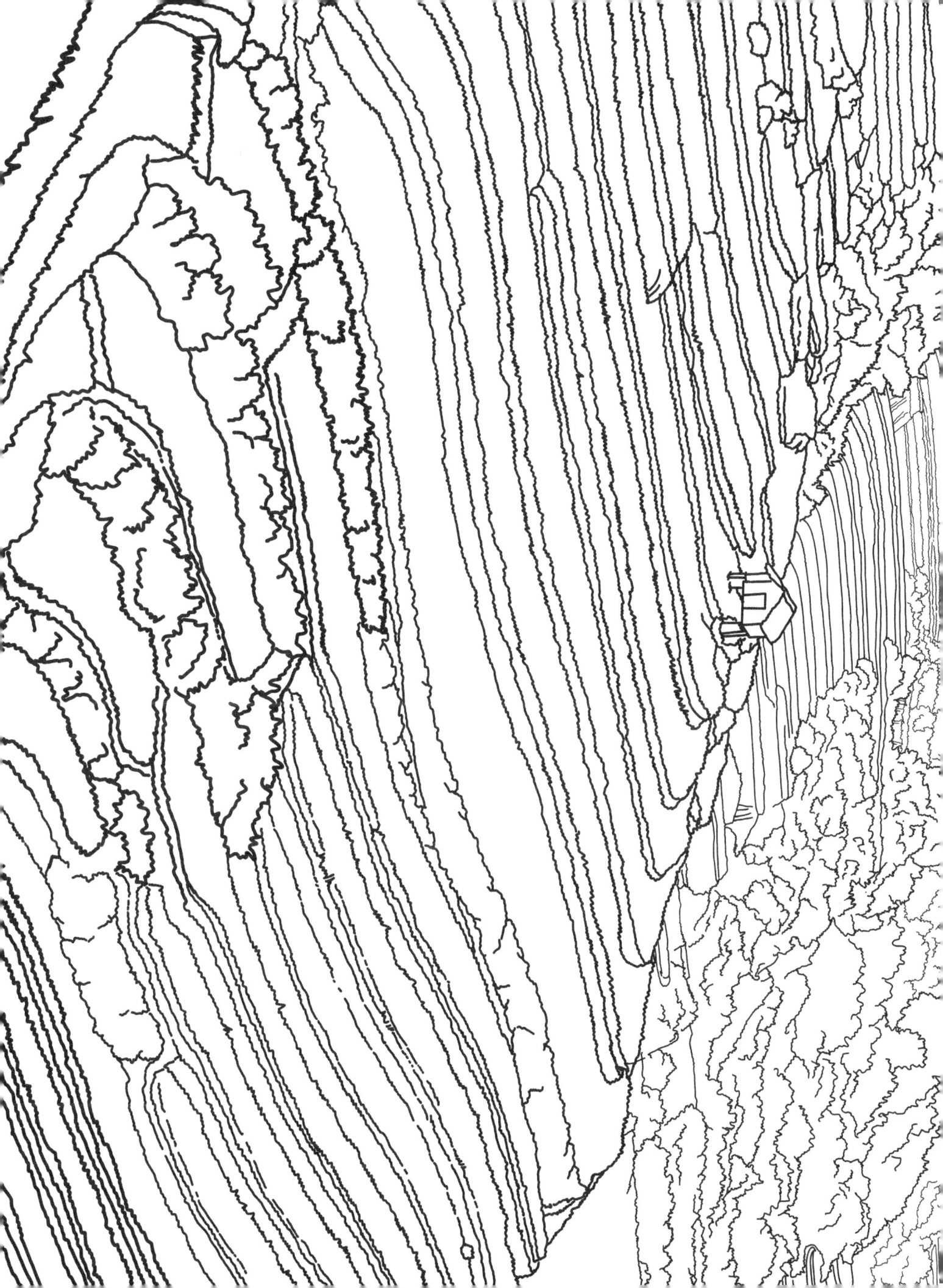

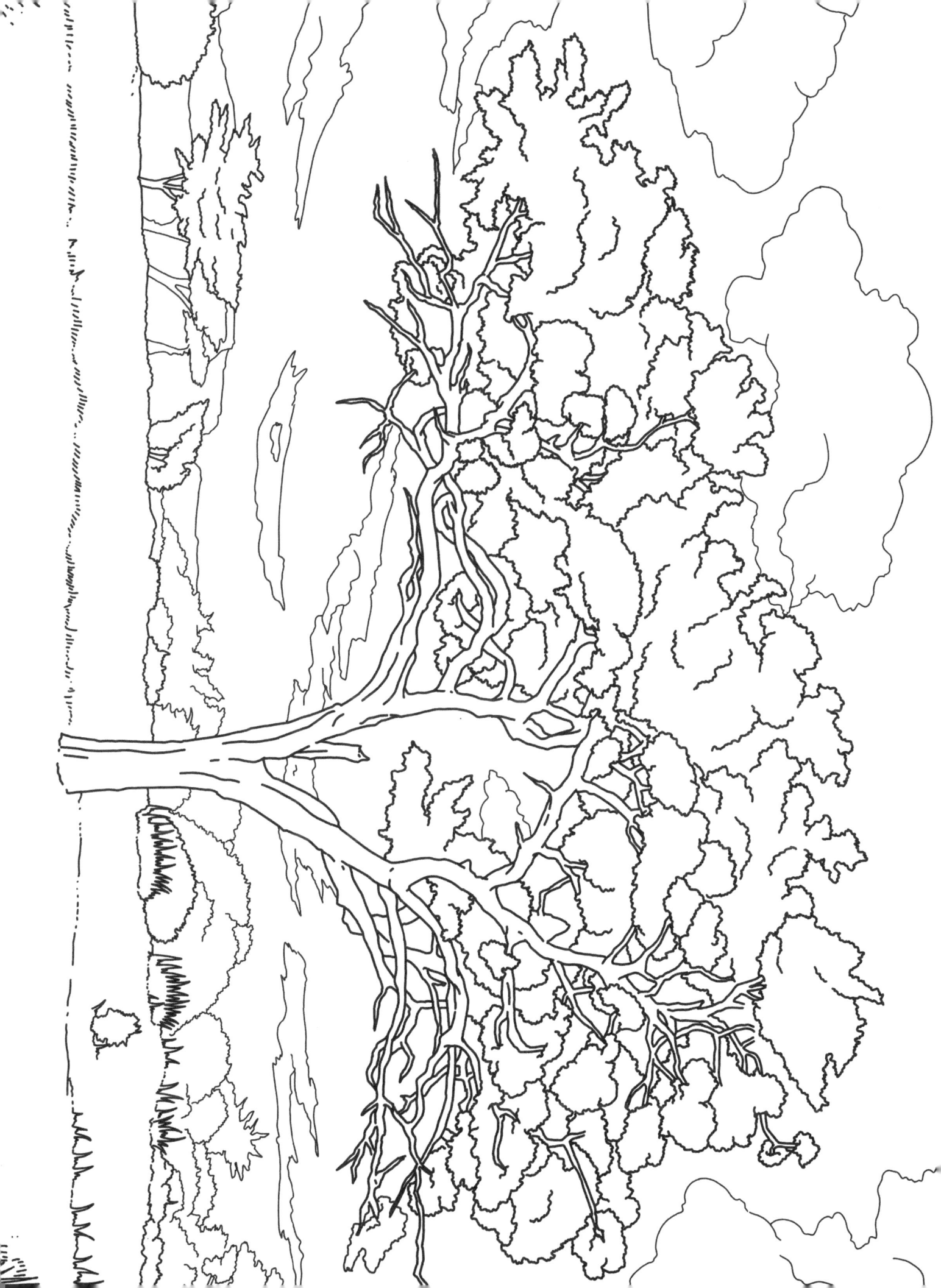

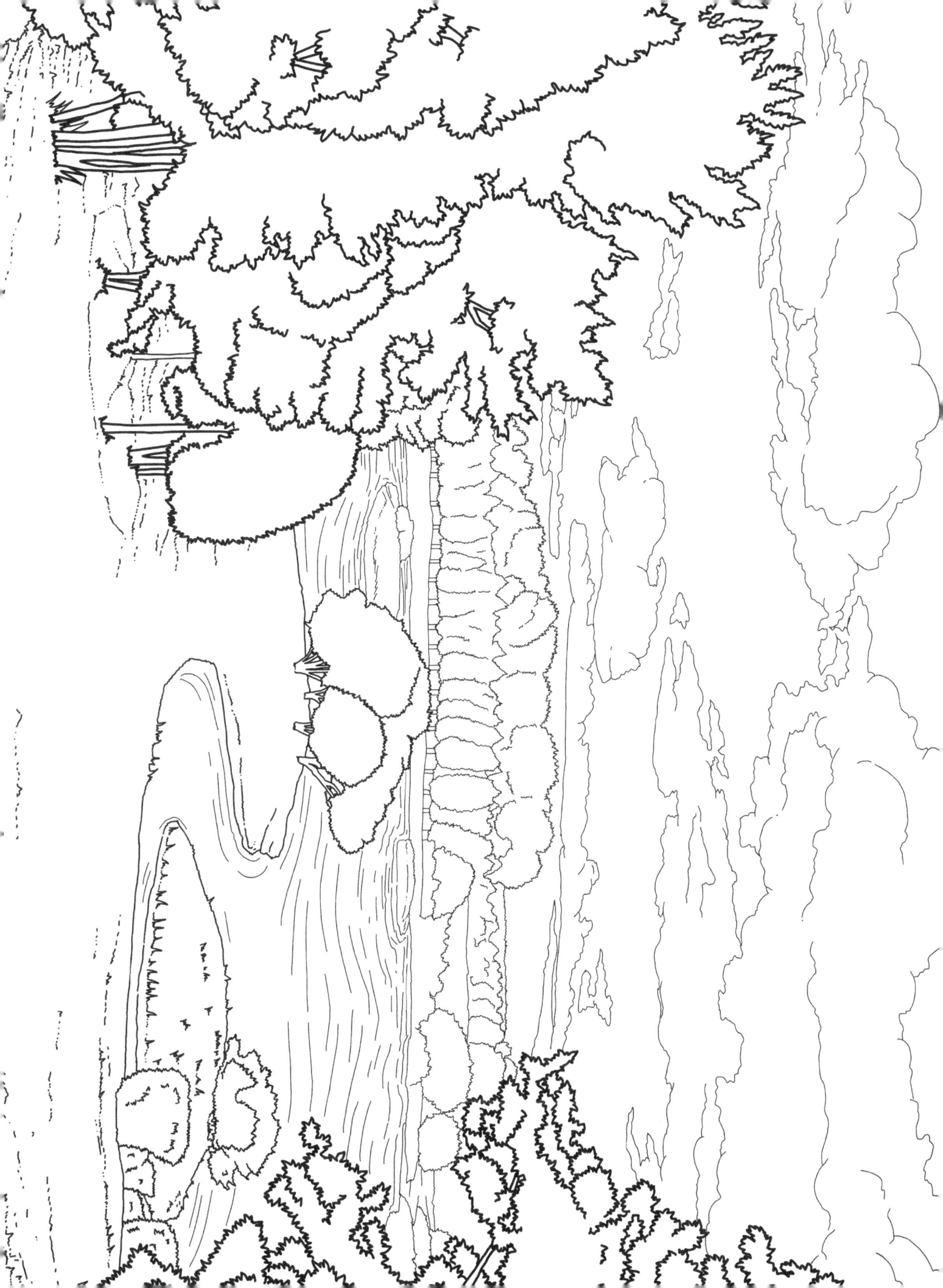

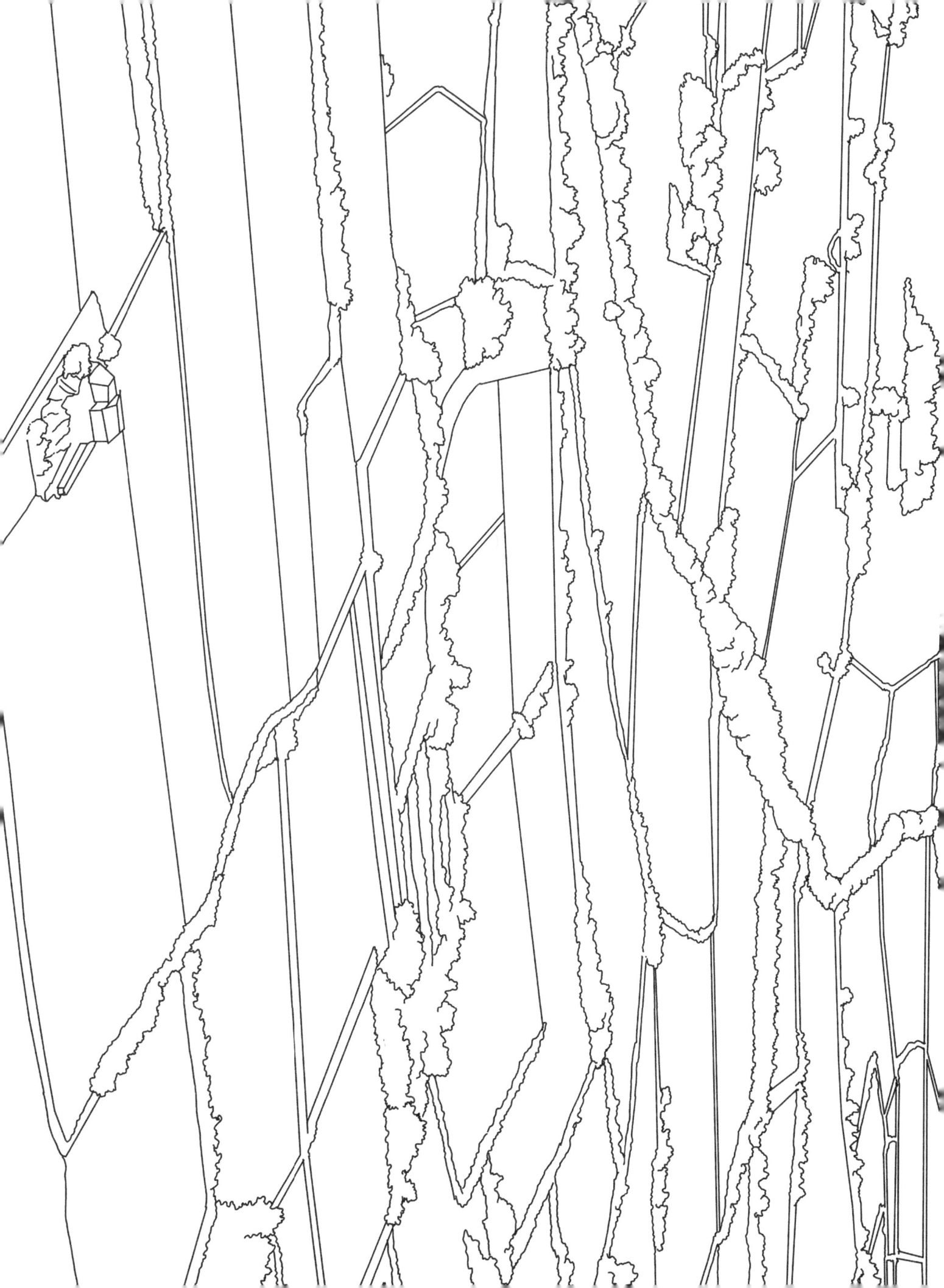

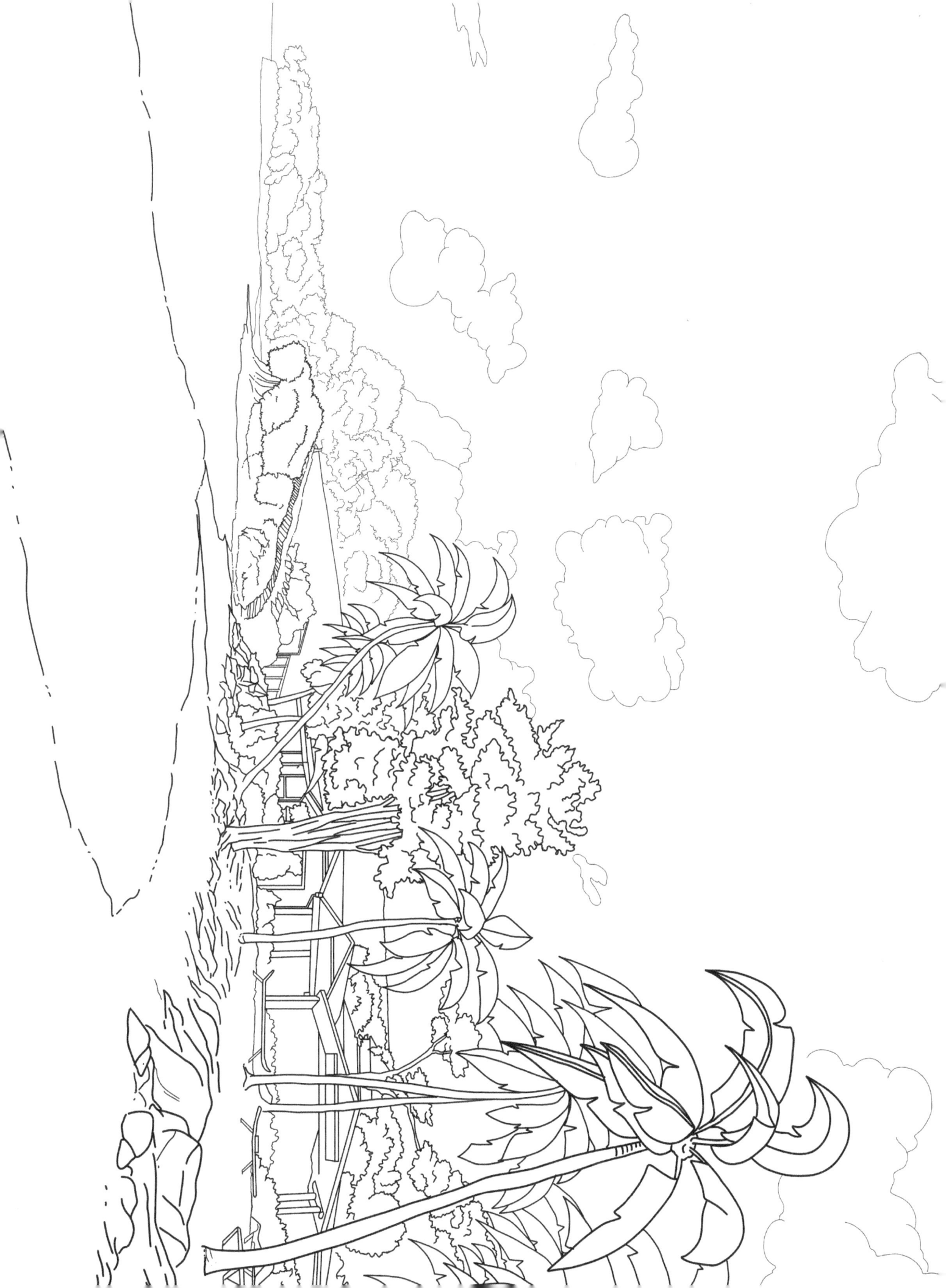

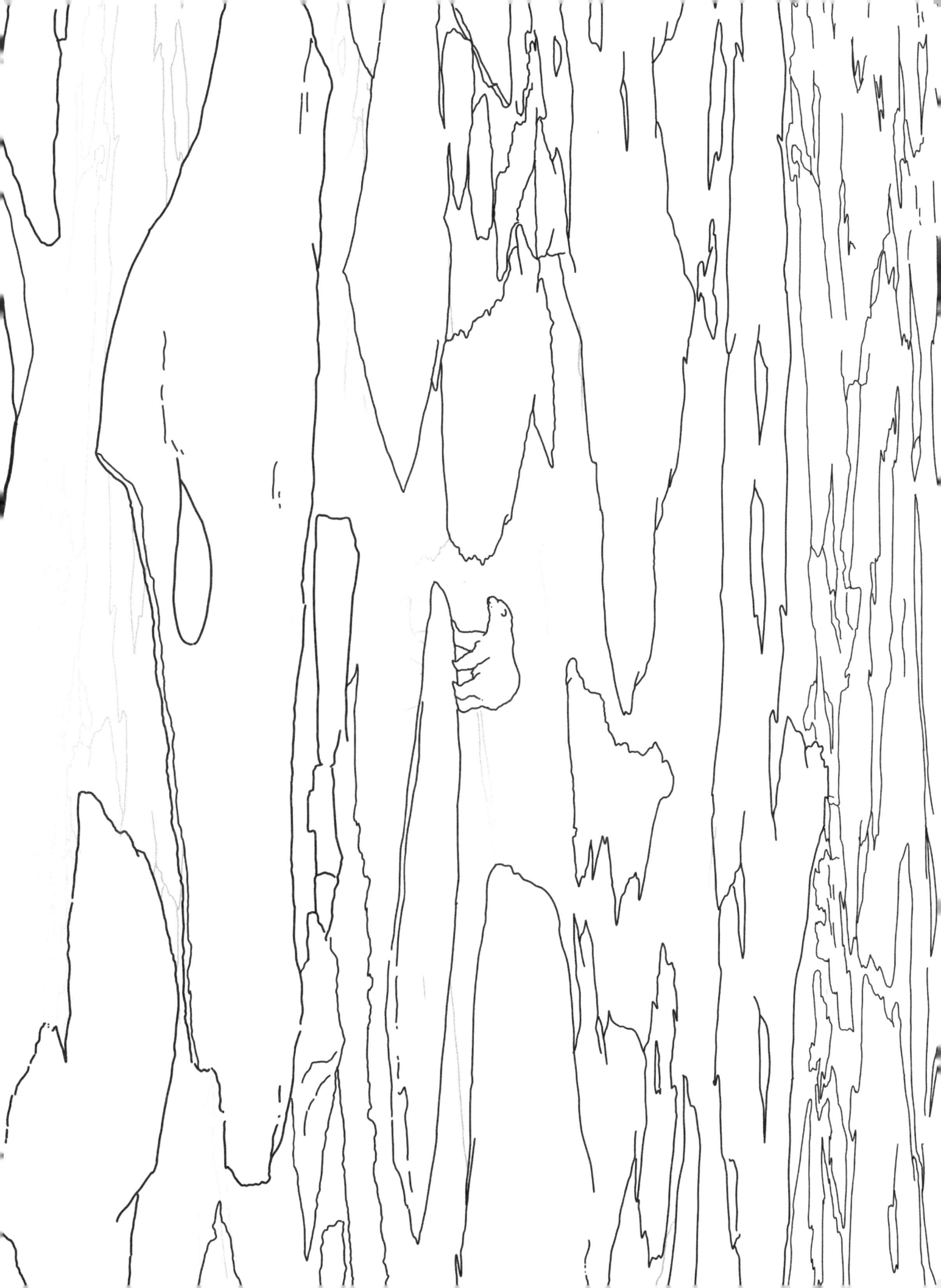

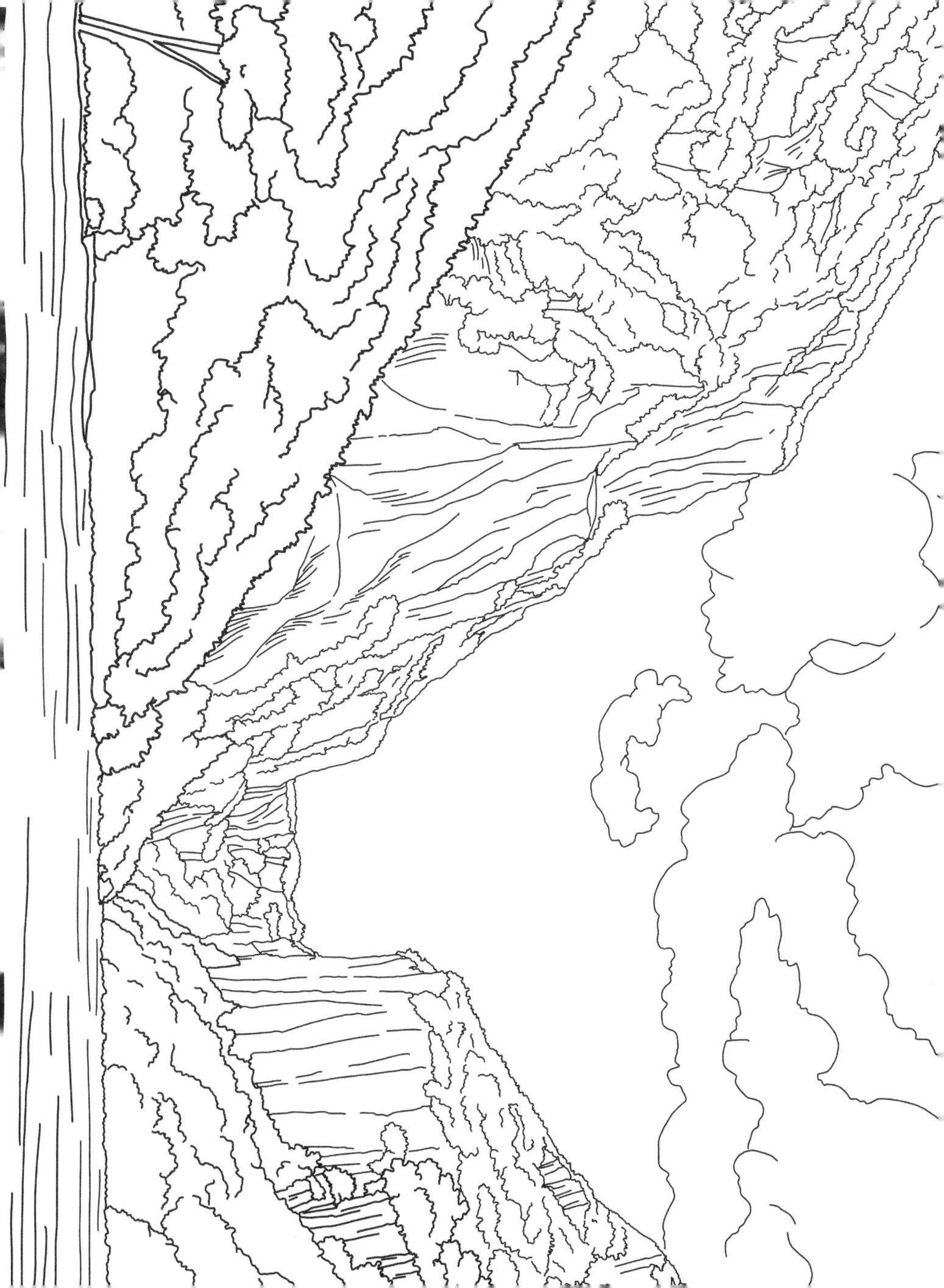

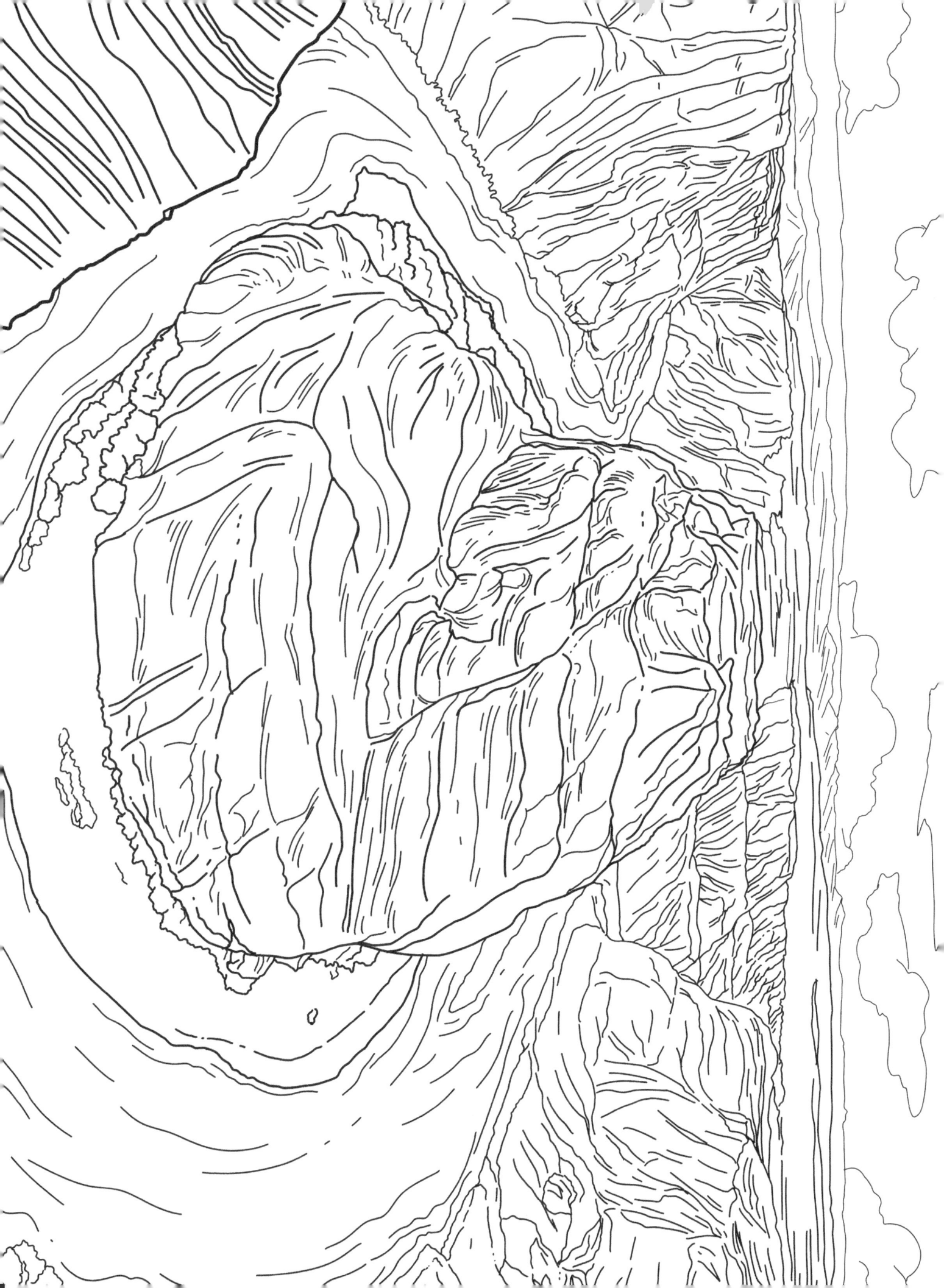

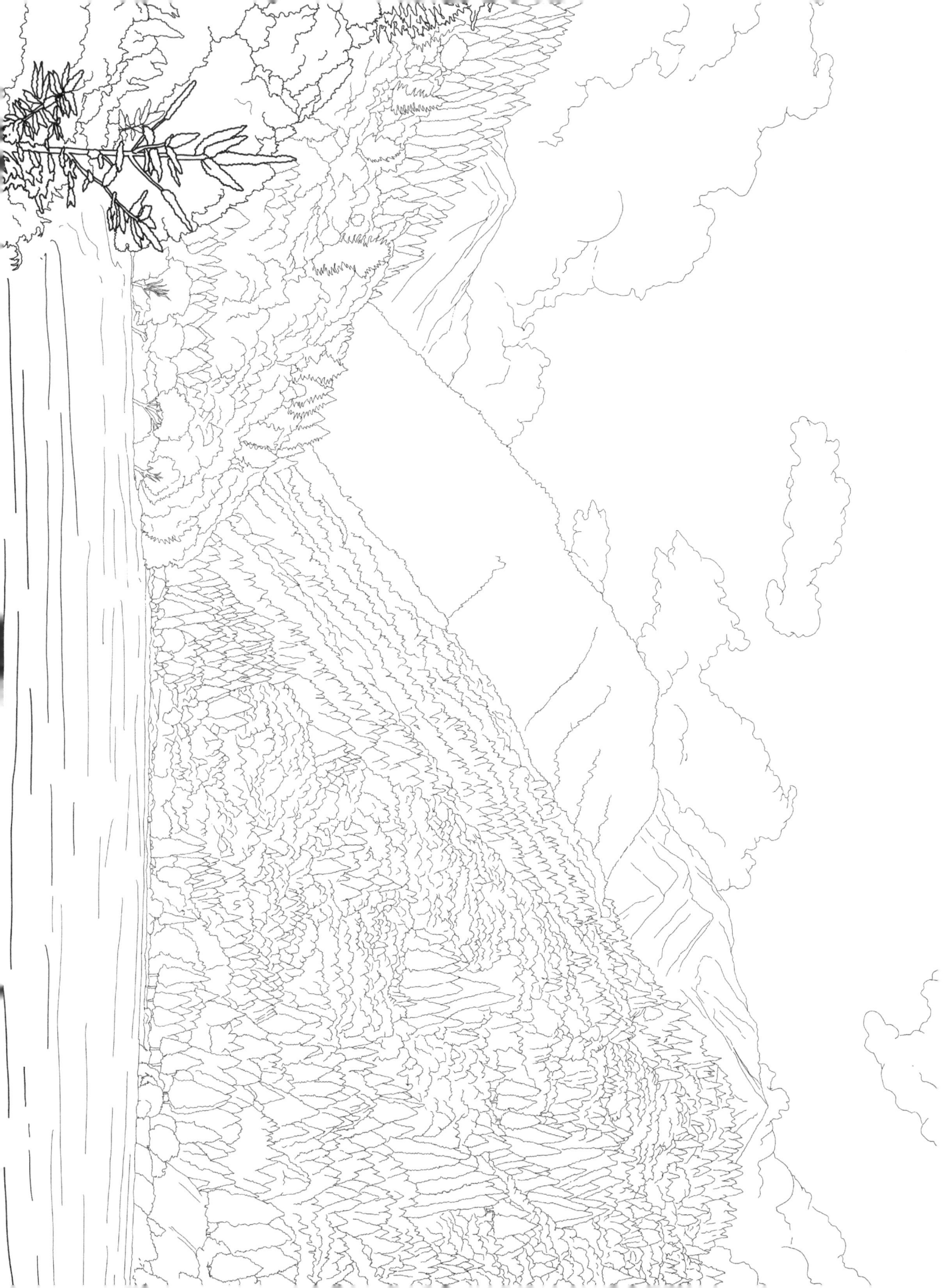

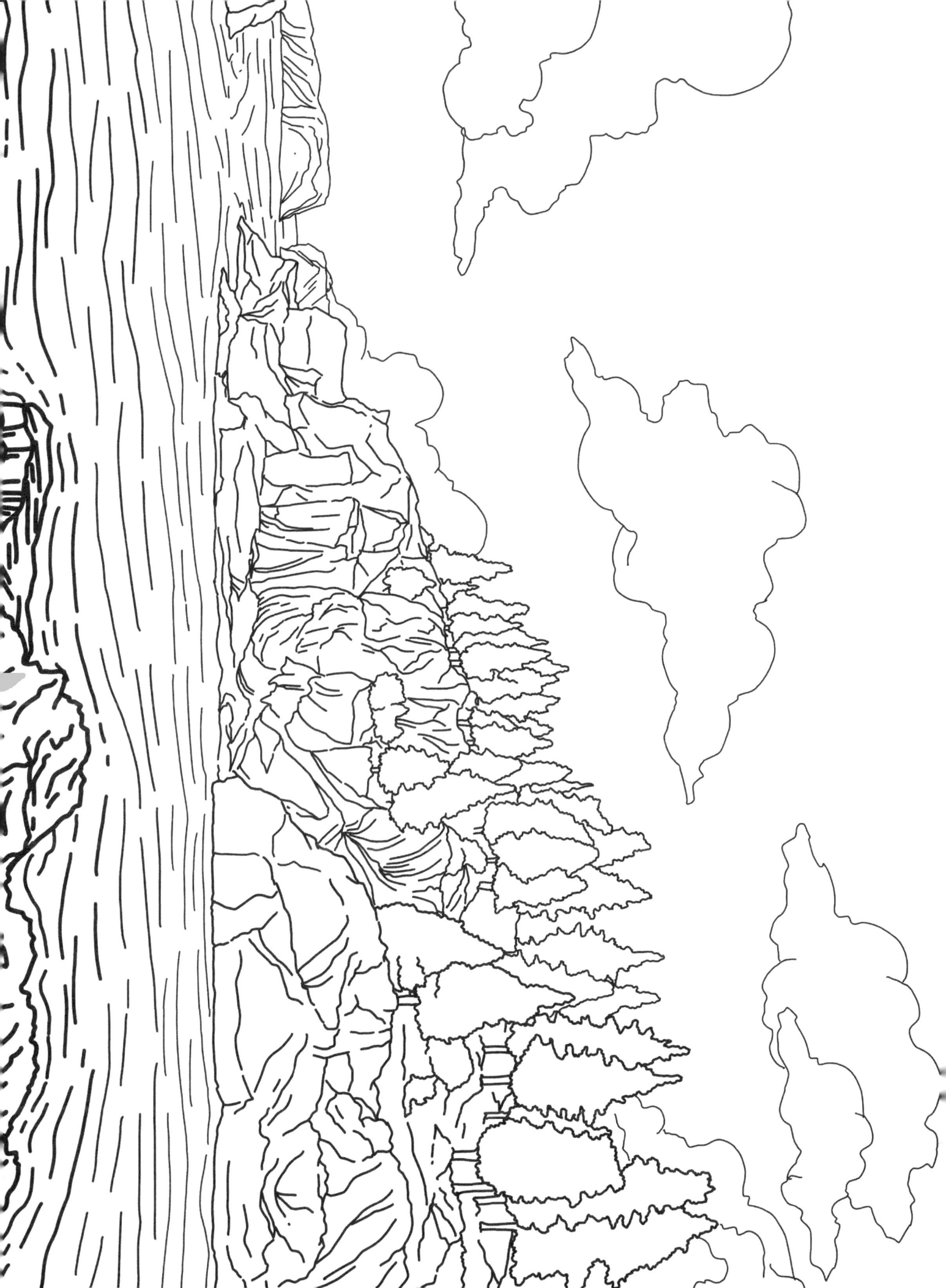

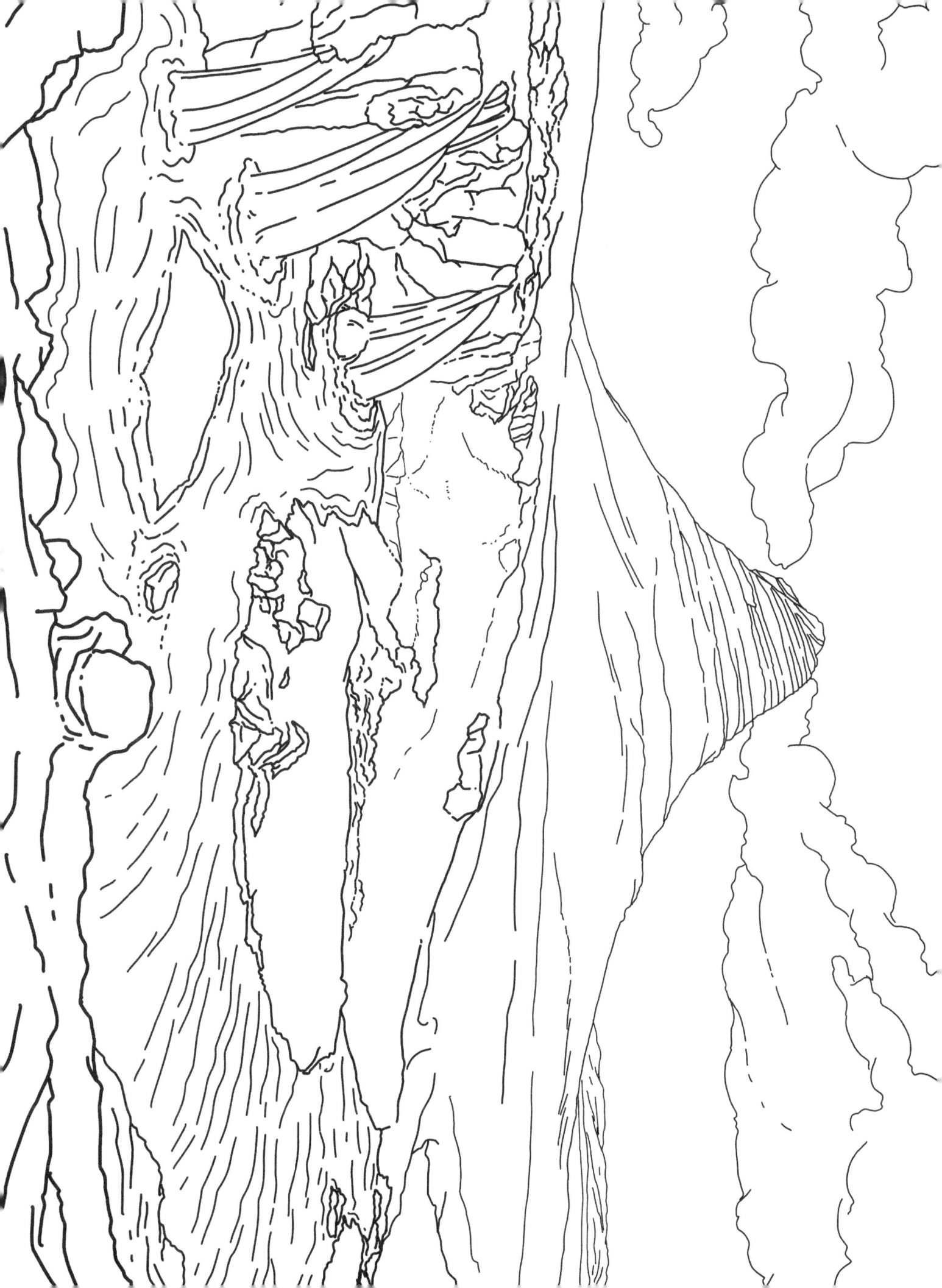

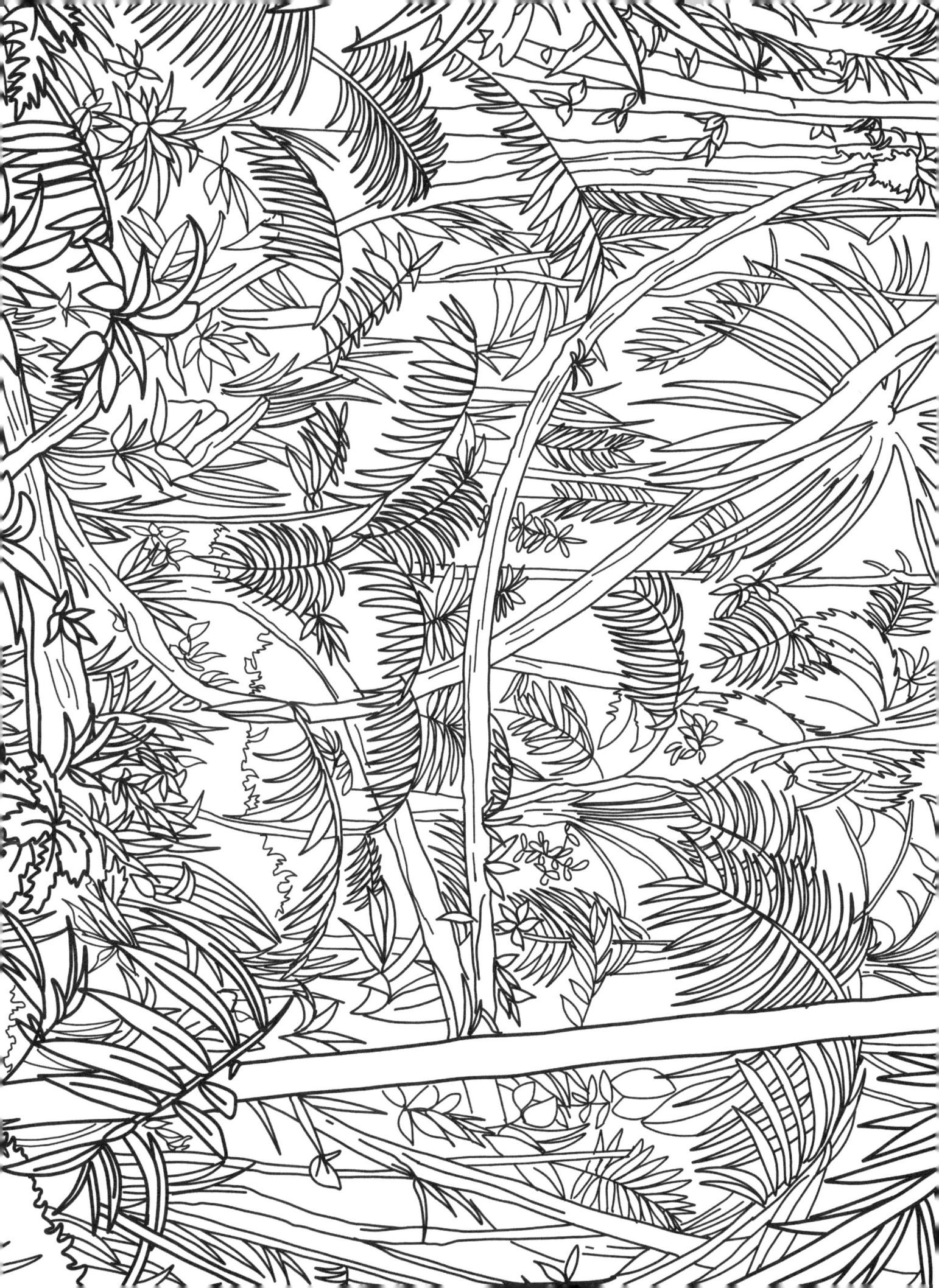

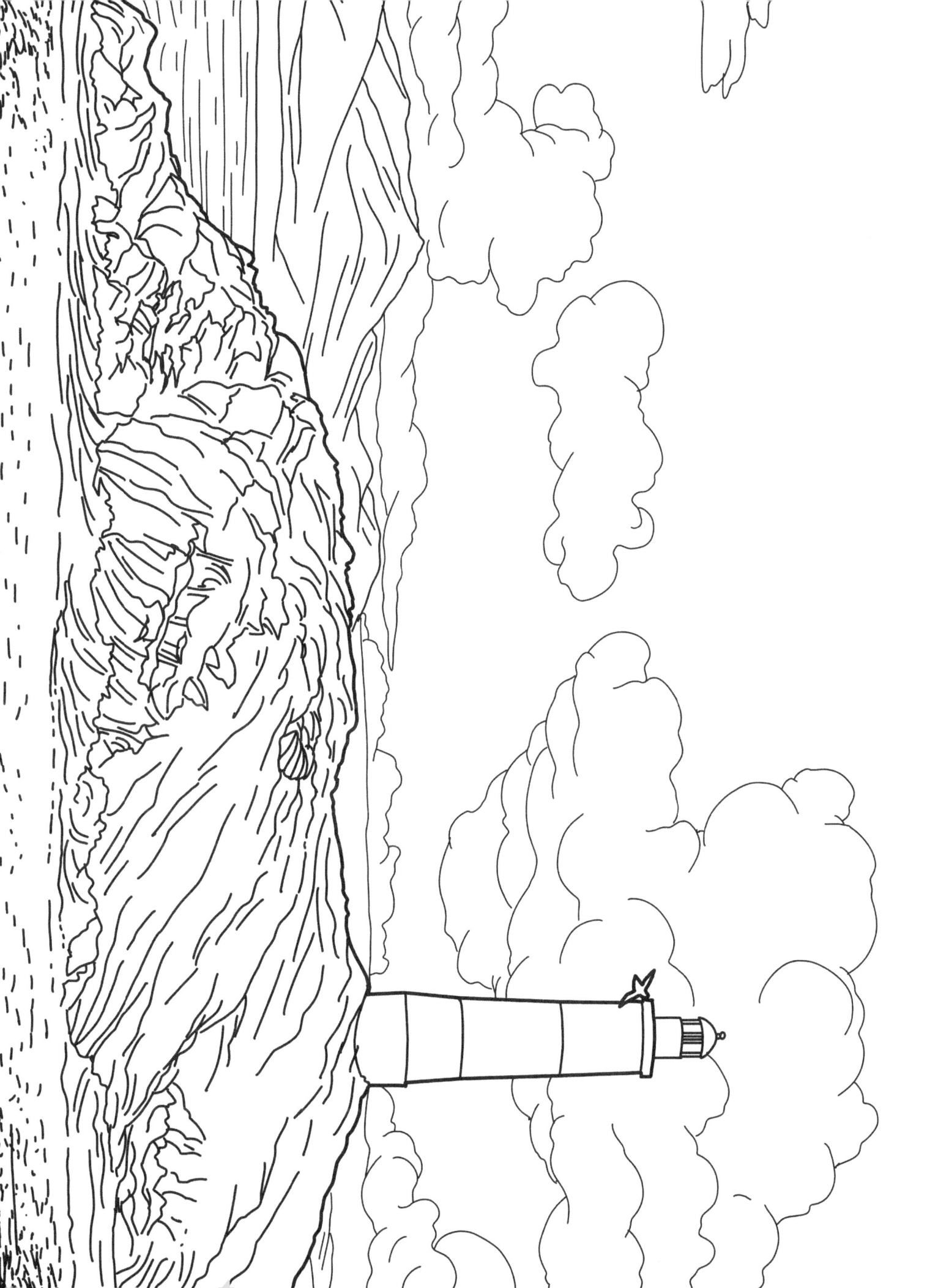

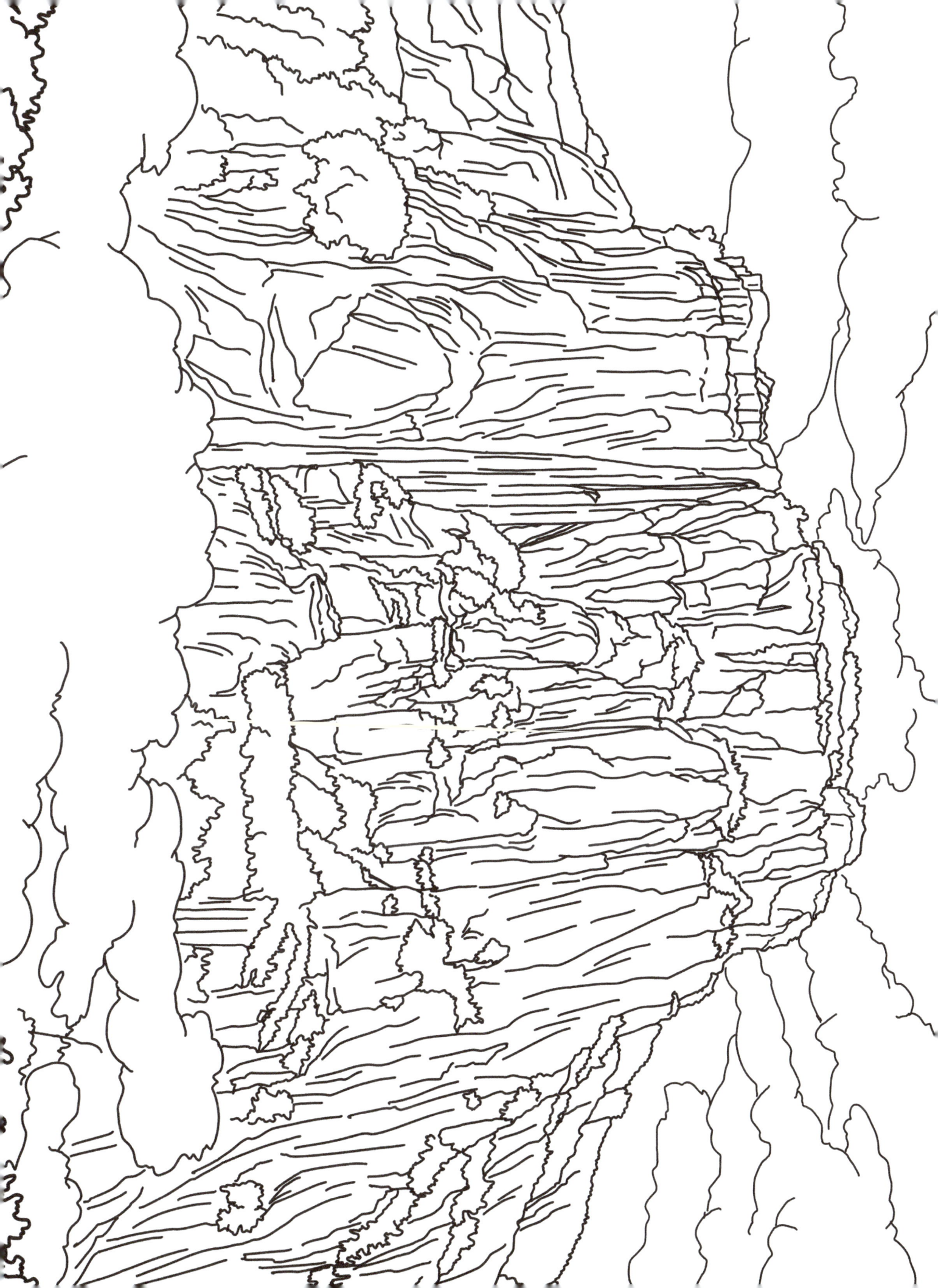

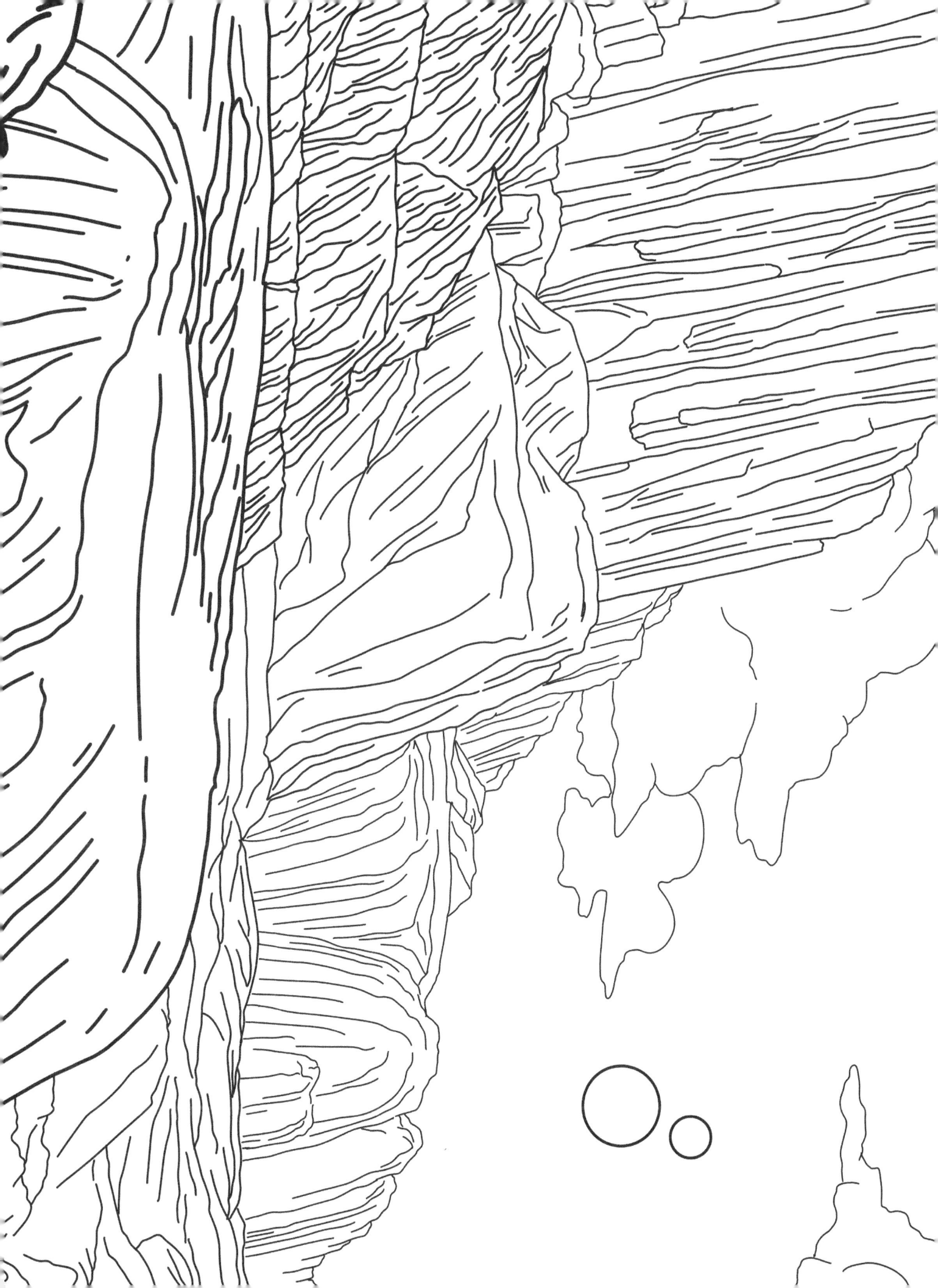

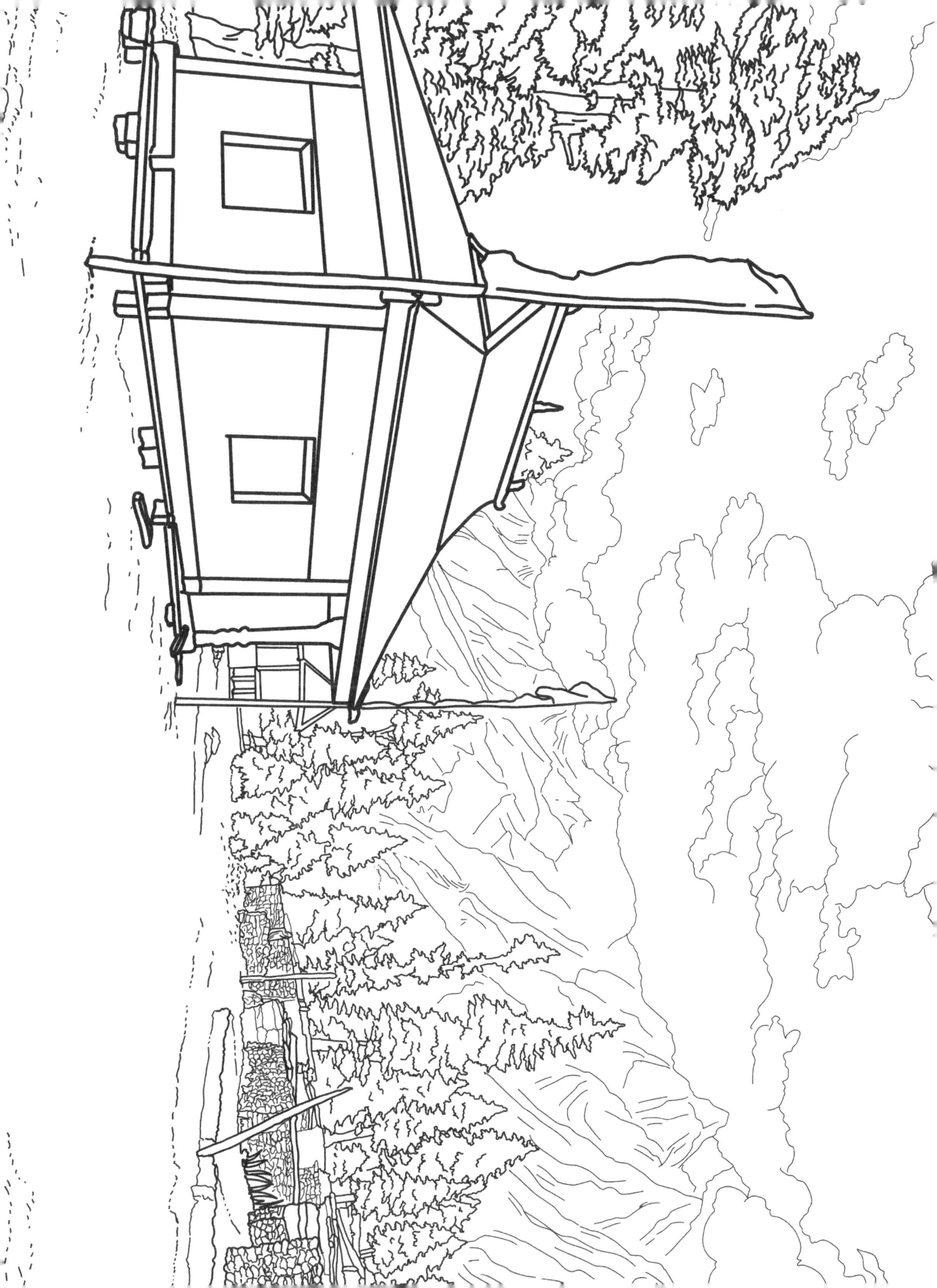

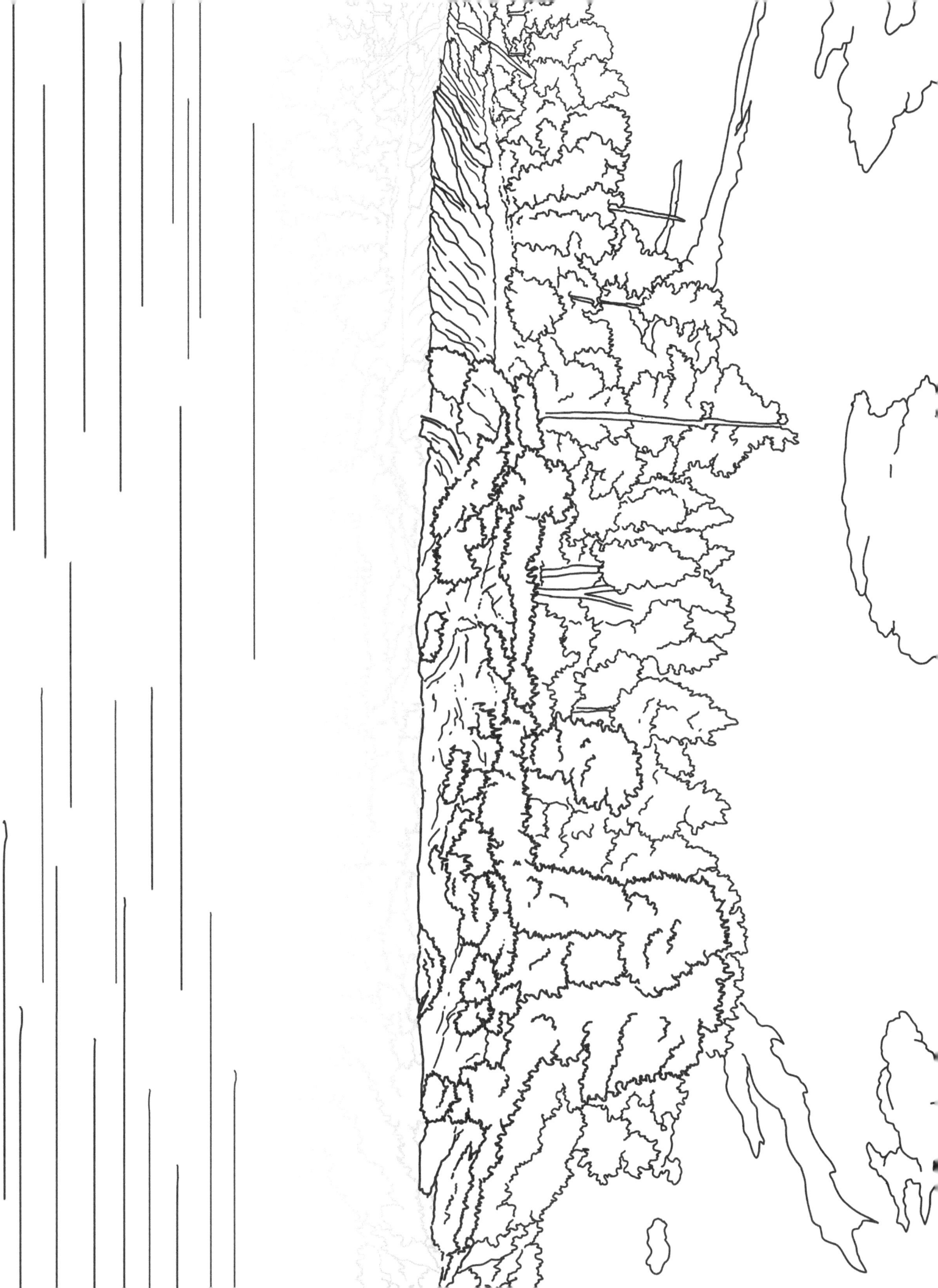

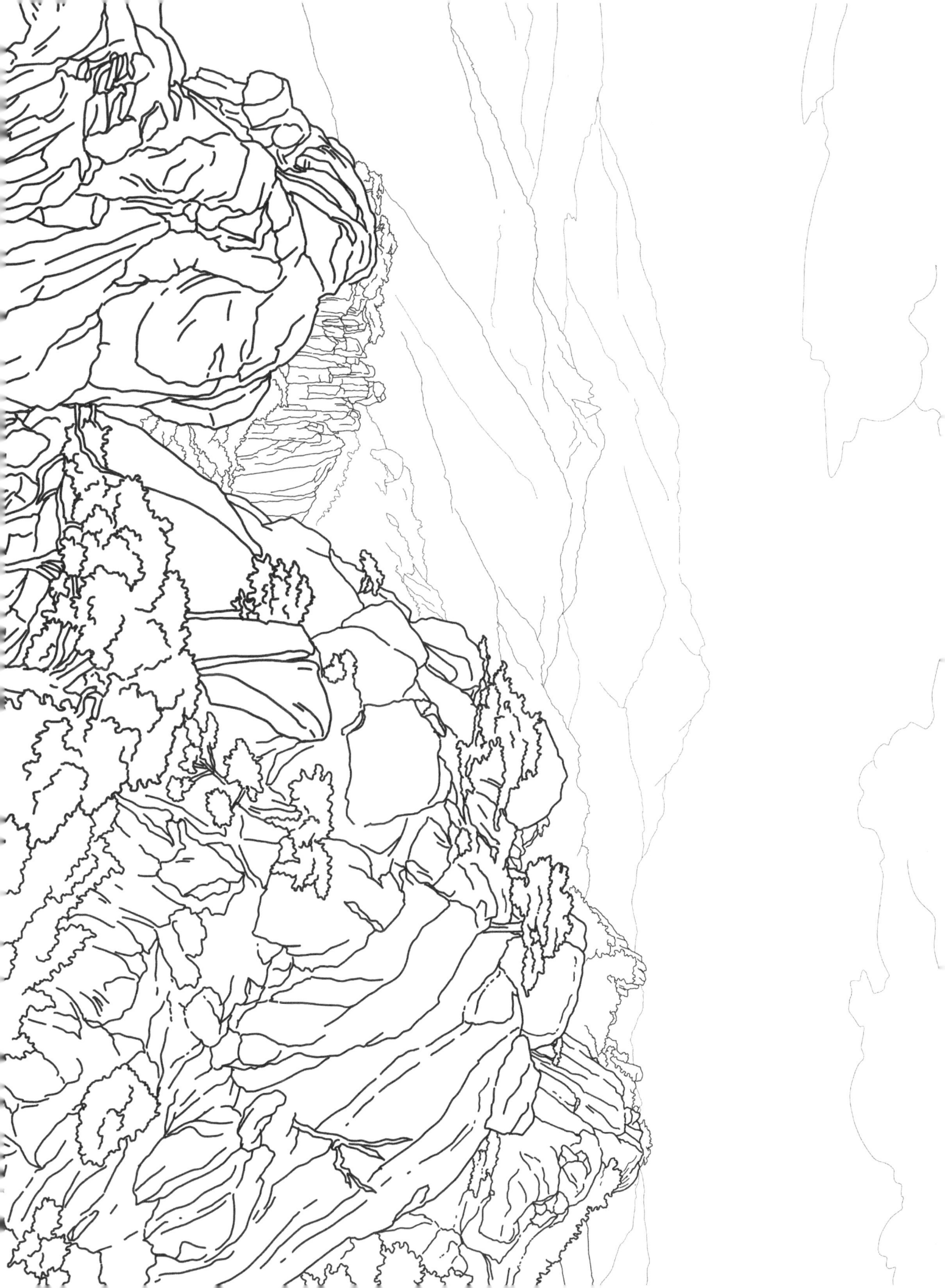

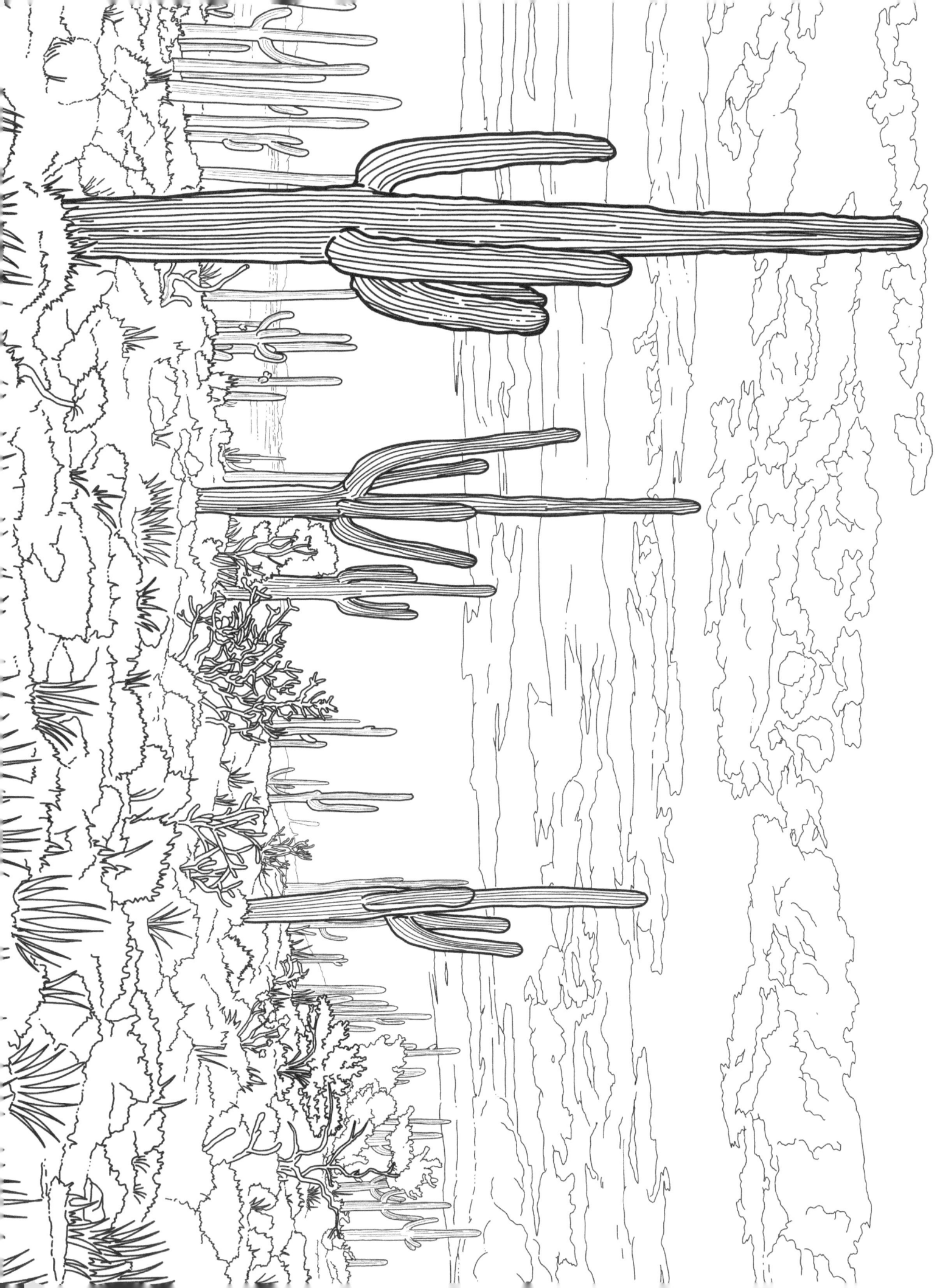

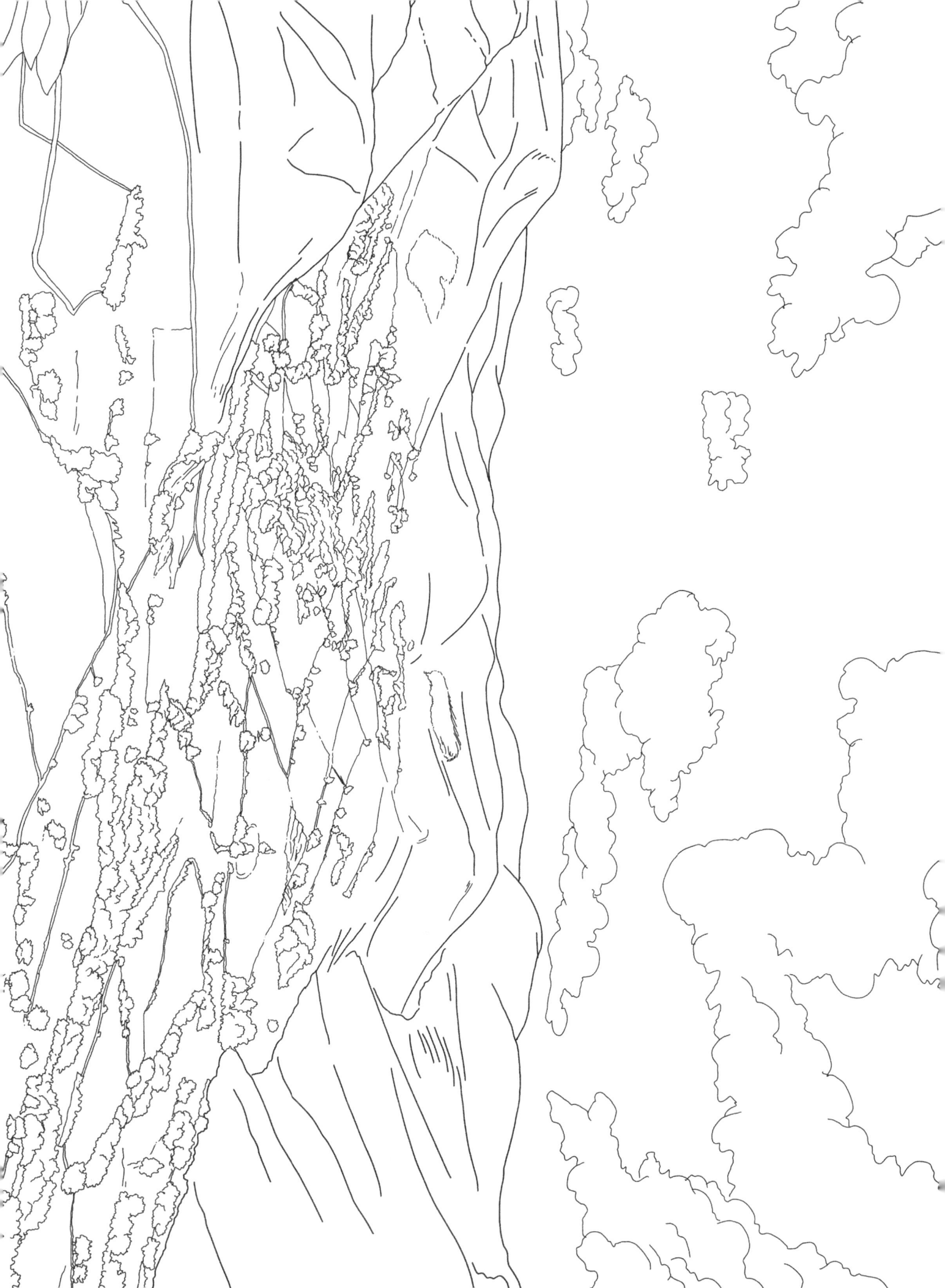

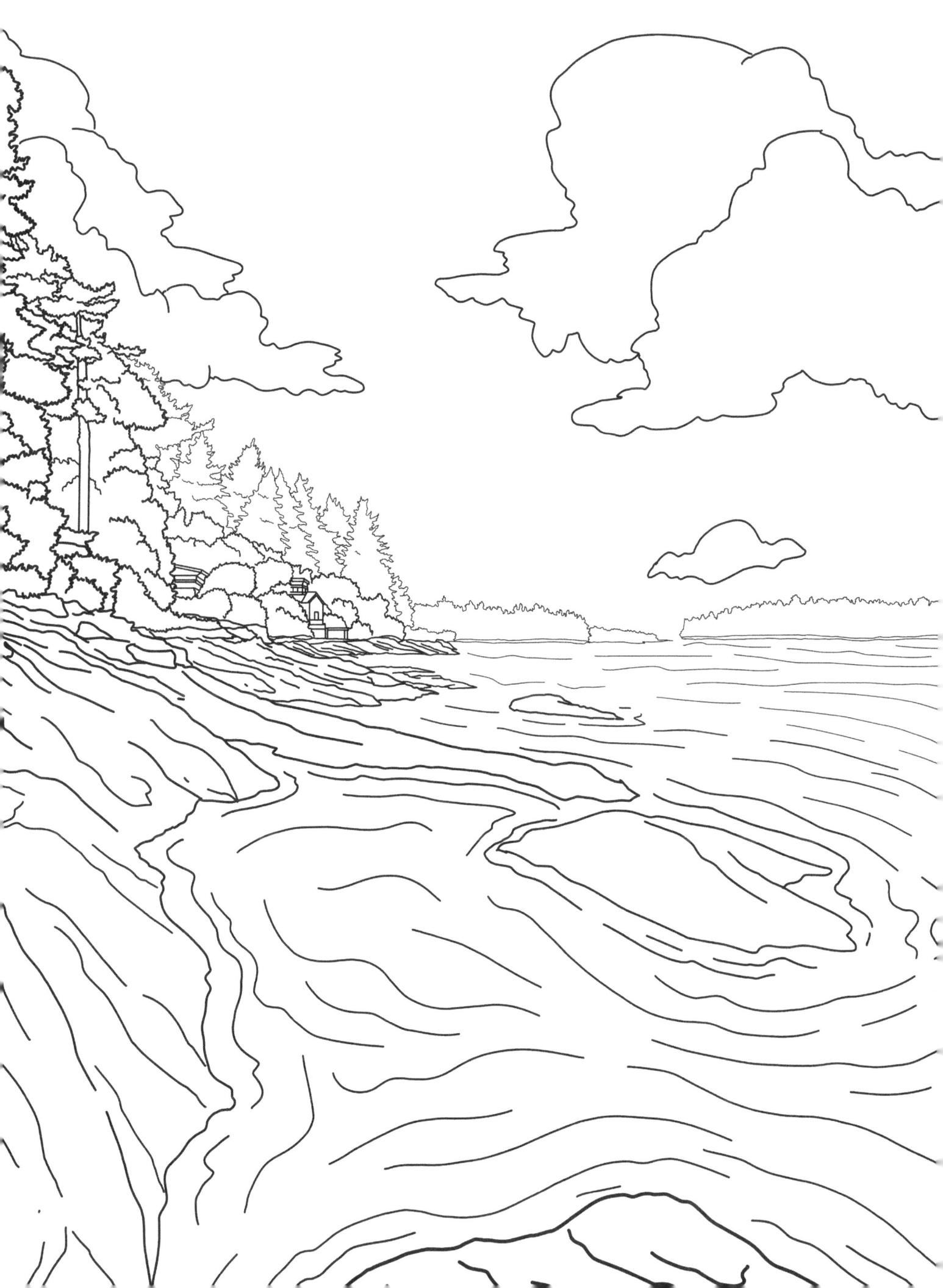

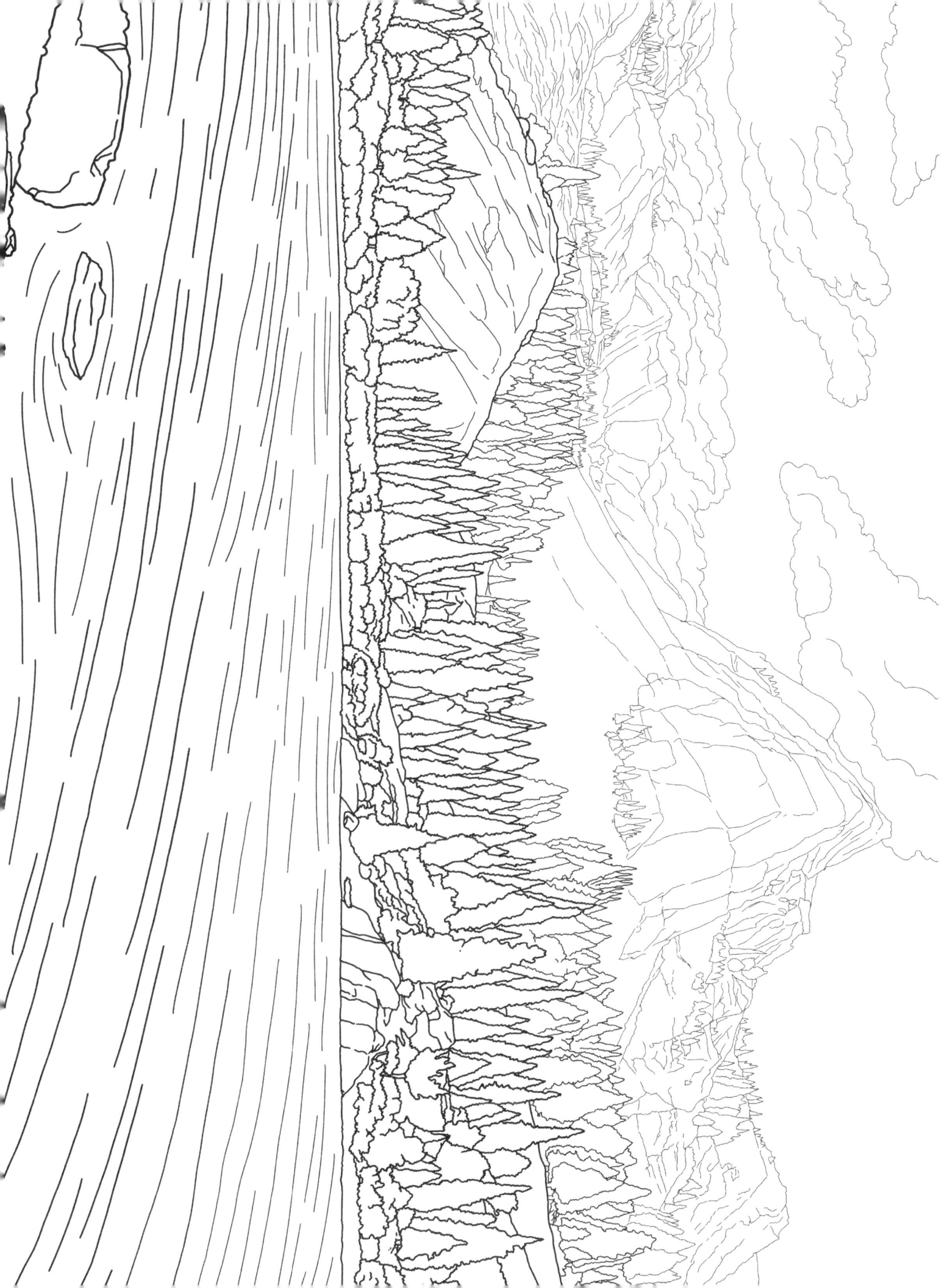

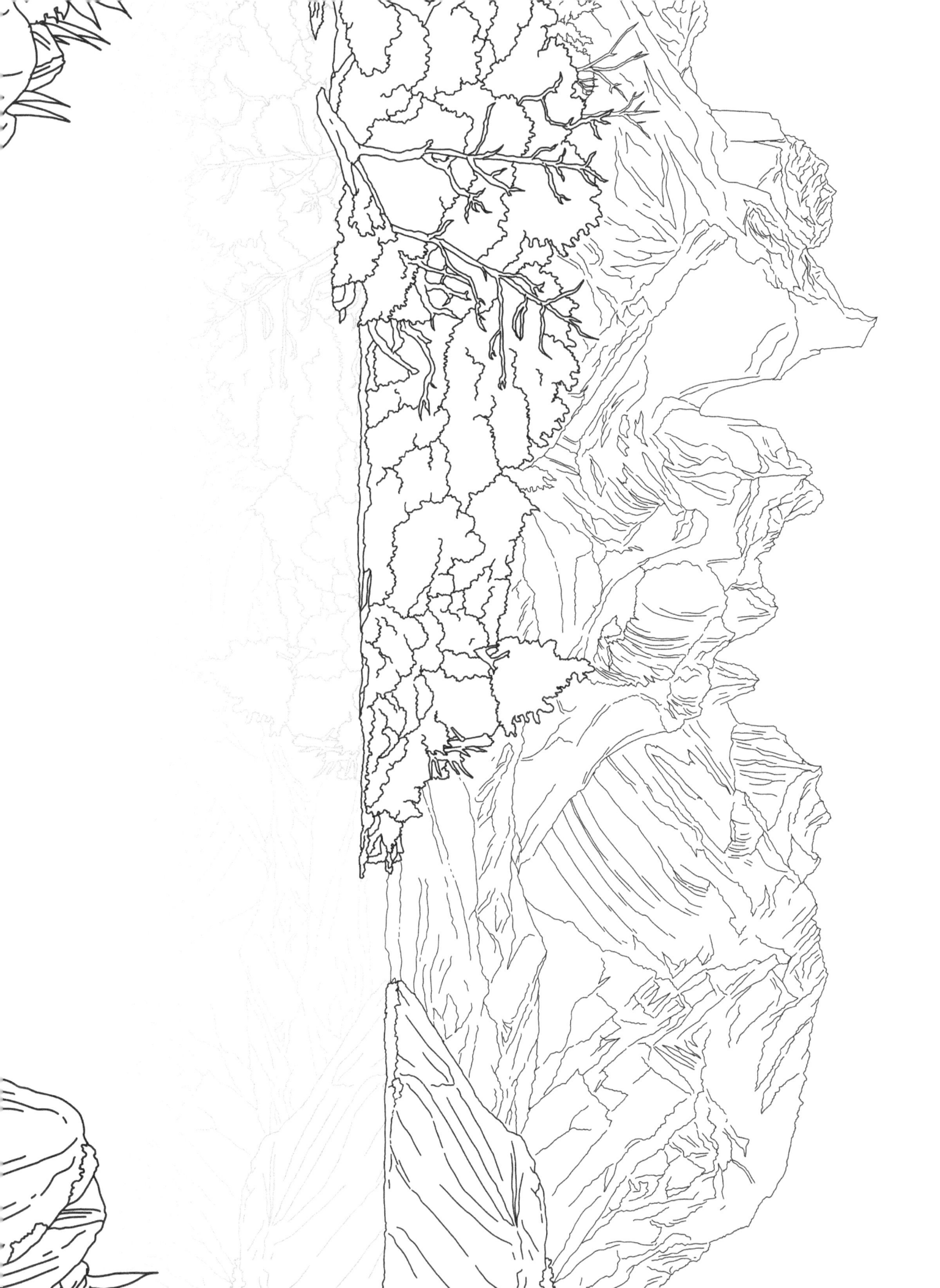

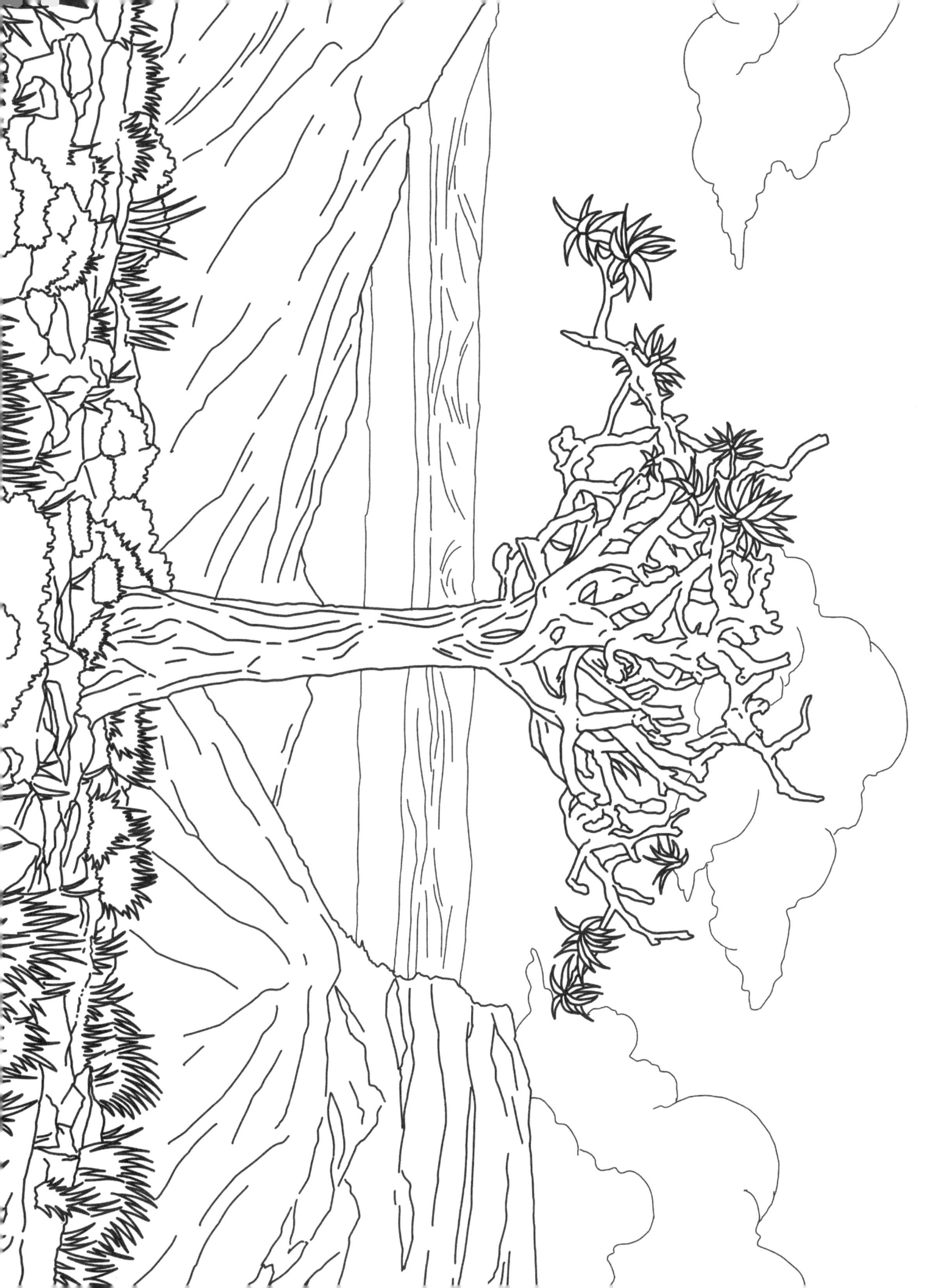

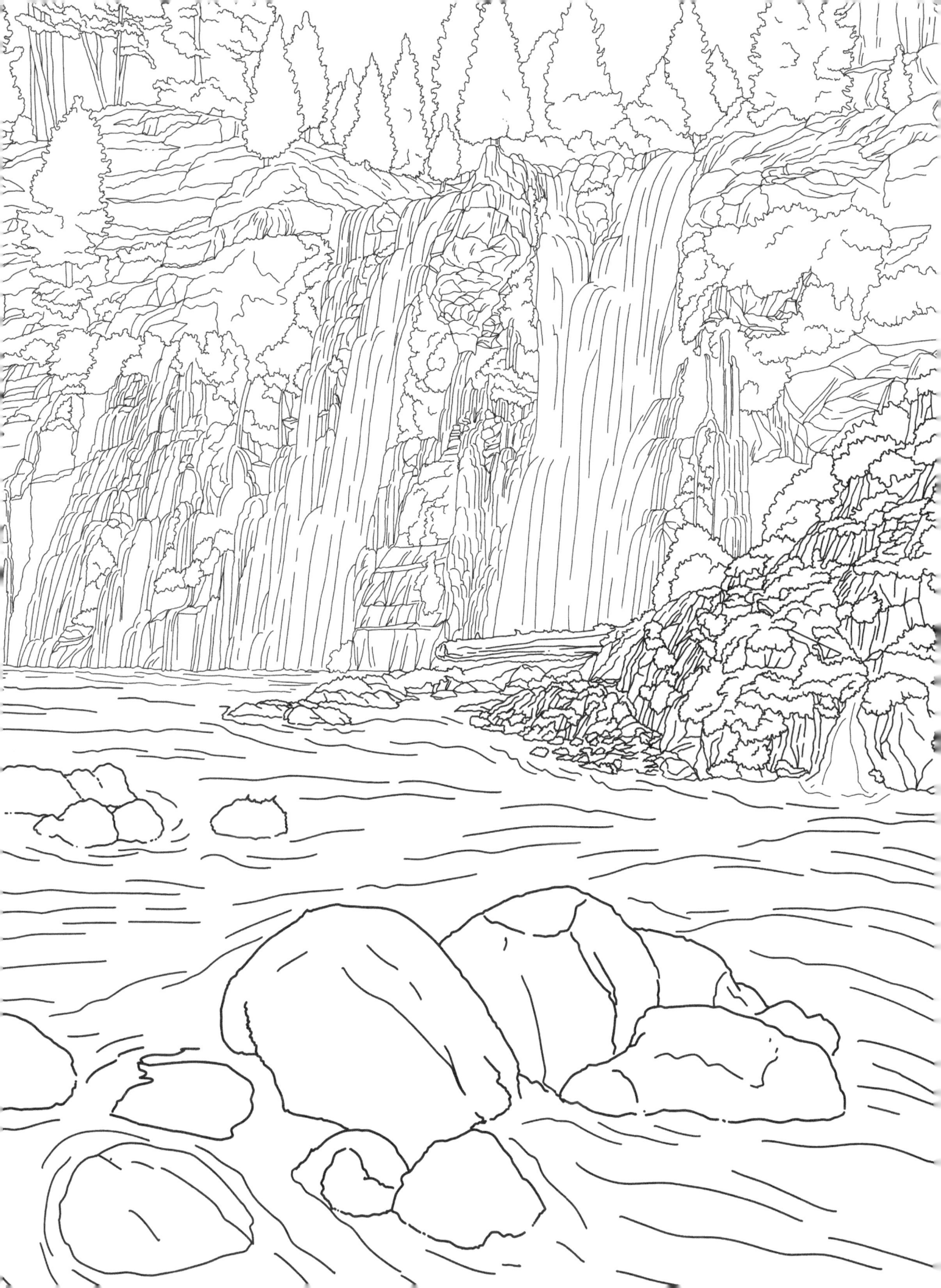

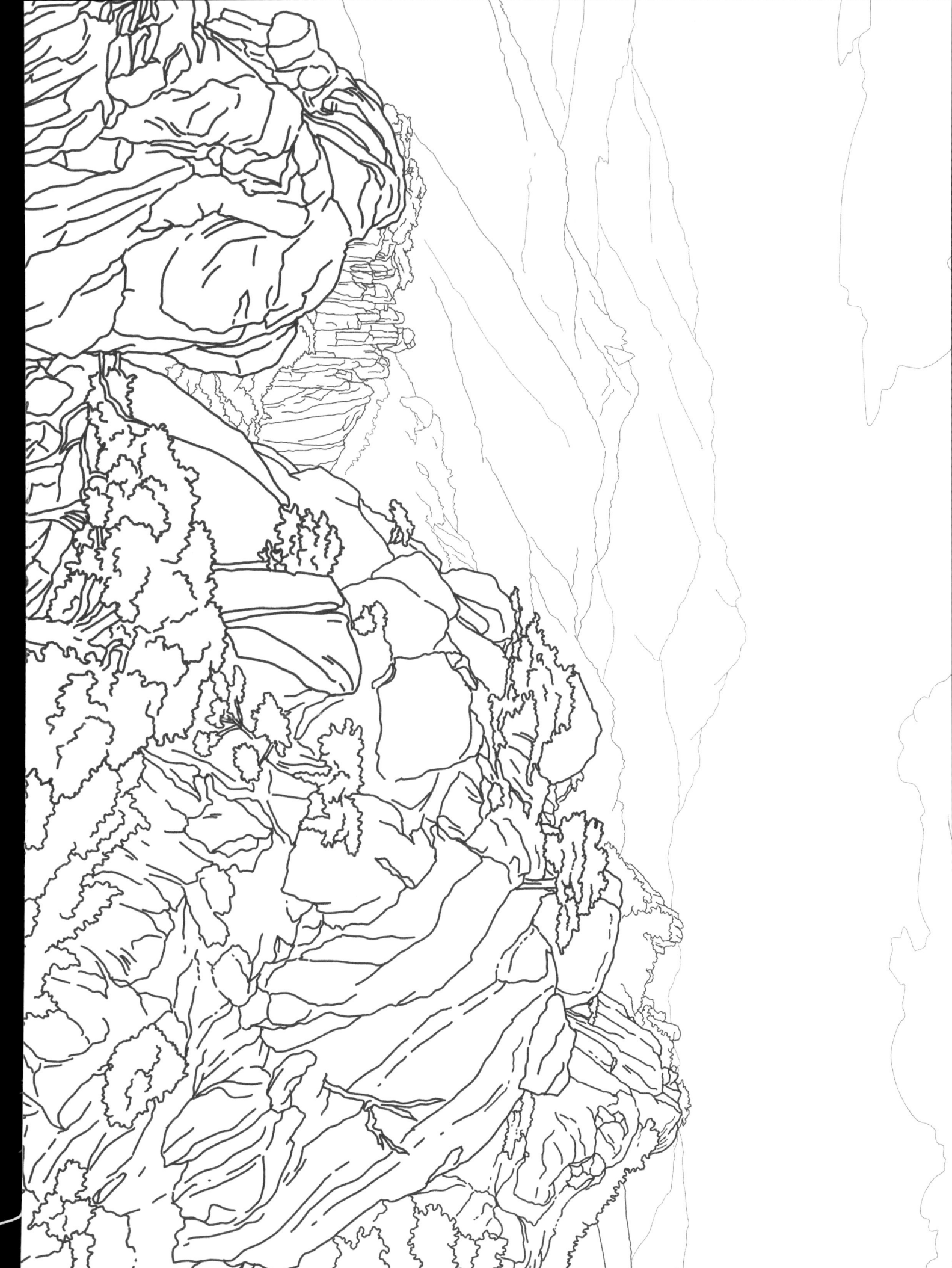